Trading Ashes for Roses:
From Pain to Passion

Connie Pombo

PublishAmerica
Baltimore

© 2005 by Connie Pombo.
All rights reserved. No part of this book may be reproduced, stored in a retrieval system or transmitted in any form or by any means without the prior written permission of the publishers, except by a reviewer who may quote brief passages in a review to be printed in a newspaper, magazine or journal.

All Scripture quotations, unless otherwise indicated, are taken from the HOLY BIBLE, NEW INTERNATIONAL VERSION®. NIV®. Copyright ©1973, 1978, 1984 by International Bible Society. Used by permission of Zondervan. All rights reserved.

Scripture quotations marked "NLT" are taken from the Holy Bible, New Living Translation, copyright 1996. Used by permission of Tyndale House Publishers, Inc., Wheaton, Illinois 60189. All rights reserved.

First printing

ISBN: 1-4137-9422-X
PUBLISHED BY PUBLISHAMERICA, LLLP
www.publishamerica.com
Baltimore

Printed in the United States of America

Note to Readers

Trading Ashes for Roses is the message that can be found in any human tragedy, pain, or loss. We get to choose what we will do with that pain—an inevitable part of life—and transform it into a life of passion—a celebration of life.

There are more than 9 million Americans today living with cancer. From the moment of diagnosis through all the stages described in this book, they are "survivors"—a word that communicates hope and healing. It is for this reason I have chosen to use the term survivor instead of patient.

I am forever grateful to all the physicians and healthcare providers who were instrumental in my recovery; however, I have chosen not to include their actual names for purposes of confidentiality. The conversations included in this book are quoted from memory.

Please note that this is my personal journey with breast cancer, and it is in no way to replace the doctor-patient relationship. This book serves to educate and inform readers on the emotional aspects related to the cancer experience.

Dedication

In loving memory

To my dear friend and "mentor in crisis,"
Juanita Hiestand,
who said,
"One day you'll trade these ashes for roses."

CONTENTS

Foreword by Katherine Bowers	9
Acknowledgments	11
Prologue *The Gift of Roses*	13
1. Shock: *What Did I Do Wrong?*	17
2. Anger: *Warning Signals*	27
3. Fear: *Can't Be Late To Radiate!*	43
4. Denial: *Going Backward Not Forward*	55
5. Depression: *The Skunk Train*	62
6. Acceptance: *The Other Side*	71
7. Living Life Passionately: *A Life Beyond Cancer*	84
Epilogue *Time Brings Roses*	91
Appendix 1: When Words Matter Most	95
Appendix 2: Helpful Things To Do	99
Appendix 3: Signs and Symptoms of Depression	103
Appendix 4: Scripture Readings	105

Appendix 5: How to Enjoy a Positive Attitude for Life	109
Resources	111
Recommended Reading	115
Works Cited	117

FOREWORD
by Katherine Bowers

What an inspiring, hope-filled, passionate, and real portrait of rich, fragrant, and vibrant roses stemming from the least likely of places—a mound of ashes. Connie Pombo is a sweet-smelling fragrance of hope, faith, and love that springs forth out of the ashes of her battle with cancer, and teaches all of us how we too can trade our ashes for roses.

For the one who is going through or has survived a deadly winter, whether it be cancer, divorce, abuse, or any of the numerous trials, *Trading Ashes for Roses*, is a story of warmth in the cold, growth in the silence, a light shining in the darkness: a revelation that even the shadows are a sign that there is a light shining somewhere nearby; hope that presses us onward and upward, onward through the winter's relentless ground, upward to once again feel the Son's warmth upon our face; a portrait of new life bursting forth from the dark and lifeless ashes of our past.

As a friend of someone who has cancer I needed this book! I could never have imagined—not in a million years—what it is like to walk that walk. I am thankful for Connie's honesty in her suffering. It has given me strength and wisdom to come alongside those who are hurting. *Trading Ashes for Roses* paints such a sweet picture of a fragile rose pushing through the bitter snow of a deadly winter.

During various suffering and trials, many an encourager and comforter has wandered into my life. I have felt the devastation of the comforter I lovingly refer to as "a bull in a china shop"! Well-intentioned, head brimming with knowledge, lips flaring with words of wisdom, they rushed to help, and—just like the man who used a hatchet to remove a fly from his friend's forehead—hacked away at the strained cords that I was clinging so tightly to.

Job's words say it best: "I have heard many things like these; miserable comforters are you all! Will your long-winded speeches never end? What ails you that you keep on arguing? I also could speak like you, if you were in my place; I could make fine speeches against you and shake my head at you. But my mouth would encourage you; comfort from my lips would bring you relief" (Job 16:2–5).

It was not until I read Connie's book, *Trading Ashes for Roses*, that I truly got a glimpse of not only the physical struggle, but the emotional roller coaster that relentlessly hurls the cancer victim from side to side, back and forth. As the pages of Connie's battle with cancer have unfolded, and her heart has been laid bare, I have grown.

I have a precious friend, Ruth, who is battling cancer. As I have watched her play tug-of-war with this relentless enemy, I have struggled. I have wrestled with what to say, what not to say, how to help, when to cry, and when to laugh.

Trading Ashes for Roses is a how-to book for all of us inexperienced gardeners who wait, watch, and pray for spring to melt the snow's painful grip. As you read through the pages of this book, my prayer is that you will be a gardener of hope, love, laughter, encouragement, and strength in the winter of someone's life.

ACKNOWLEDGMENTS

This book is a celebration of almost a decade of living beyond cancer and learning to live life passionately, and to all those who showed me how to live it:

My loving family—my husband, Mark, and sons, Jeremy and Jonathan—who loved me when I needed to be loved the most, who cheered me on with their "I told you so's," and who made the journey so much sweeter.

My extended family and spiritual mentors, who lit the path and showed me the way when I couldn't see the light.

My breast cancer mentors—Juanita and Tricia—who are now in their heavenly home—rejoicing with the angels. They showed me by their example what a life *beyond* breast cancer looks like.

My wonderful doctors, who put up with a sometimes strong willed and very stubborn patient, especially Dr. "G," who was the first to extend his hand of healing to me and recognize me as a person and not just a disease, and whose healing words of hope were my first steps to recovery.

My editor friend, Gregg Dubbs, who first encouraged me with the thought that I should be writing full time. I quit my day job to pursue my passion—thank you!

My dear friend and joy mentor, Sheri, who has traveled her own journey of breast cancer. You are the reason I'm writing this book now—your courage through all the stages of cancer has been an inspiration to me and so many others.

My "CLASSY" writer's group and Women's Mentoring Ministries Network of Speakers for your ongoing support, strength, and creative genius.

My church family—too numerous to mention—who supported me with their love and prayers during this journey.

My heartfelt thanks to Joni Eareckson Tada for her inspiring words of encouragement, gracious spirit, and faithful testimony to the world of a life transformed from pain into passion.

And last, but certainly not least, Katherine Bowers, who said to me, "People want this book—so get busy and write it, girl!"

PROLOGUE

THE GIFT OF ROSES

He will give beauty for ashes, joy instead of mourning, praise instead of despair. For the LORD has planted them like strong and graceful oaks for his own glory.
—Isaiah 61:3 NLT

Roses—who can resist them? They represent love, beauty, and gratitude. But for me the rose represents so much more. it has become a symbol of hope in the midst of pain and suffering.

I was 40 years old when I was diagnosed with breast cancer—nearly a decade ago. I stumbled through the predictable stages of cancer until I fell into the ugly pit of depression. Climbing out of that despair led me into a passionate joy for living—a celebration of life. Shortly after I was diagnosed, my dear friend and joy mentor, Juanita Hiestand, said to me, "One day you'll trade these ashes for roses." It would be years before I understood the meaning behind those words, but they helped me find my way to a life beyond breast cancer.

In every chapter of this book there is a rose—you may have to look to find it. (Or as my dear friend who likes to joke with me says, "Is this like finding Waldo?") No! But you may have to do some digging. Throughout my cancer journey, God was very near to me.

Although at times I couldn't feel His presence—He was there.

I am not a "master gardener," but I know that roses take a lot of TLC. They have to be pruned, mulched, sprayed, and fertilized to produce healthy roses. In fact, one of the secrets to growing beautiful roses is the use of ashes as nutrients in the soil. And not just ordinary ashes, but those burned from hardwood in the fireplace on a cold winter's night. It's not surprising to me that roses would thrive in such a rich mixture of conditions. And so it is with our lives—the ashes of pain and loss have the potential of transforming our lives into a beautiful bouquet of roses—an enduring fragrance of God's eternal love.

Trading Ashes for Roses is the account of my personal journey with cancer—from the first painful days of diagnosis to my present ministry of sharing with others how they too can live the passionate life. Pain is pain—whether physical, mental, spiritual, or emotional—but how we are transformed by it, is our message to the world.

Transforming pain into passion is my gift to anyone hurting from the loss caused by life's unexpected tragedies. I share helpful hints for the survivor, caregiver, family, and friends about how to help along each passage of the journey. I've included excerpts from my journal during each stage of cancer. These stages make up the chapters of this book.

A list of helpful do's and don'ts, websites, and organizations for cancer are found in the Appendix, along with healing words and Scripture that started me on my road to recovery and living life passionately.

This is the book I always wanted to have while I was going through cancer. I wanted to say to others, "Here, read this book—this is what I'm feeling and this is how you can help."

Blessings on this remarkable journey!

For our light and momentary troubles are achieving for us an eternal glory that far outweighs them all.
—II Corinthians 4:17

ONE

SHOCK: WHAT DID I DO WRONG?

O My God, I cry out by day, but you do not answer...
—Psalm 22:2

"What did I do wrong?" I cried out. The surgeon spoke in subdued tones, quoting statistics and survival rates, but I stopped listening. Fear drowned out his words: *This can't be happening to me.* None of it seemed real. I was in shock!

The surgeon delivered the bad news and hung up—a dial tone filled the silence. Panic seized my body. I felt smothered—unable to breathe. I let go of the phone and oceans of tears fell freely. In between sobs, I would catch a breath and repeat the words, "What did I do wrong?"

I glanced over my shoulder, and there was Mark, my husband of 20 years. His expression was hidden—hands cupped over his face. I moved slowly toward him. His arms reached out to hold me tightly against his chest as if to protect me from the fear that seized my body. When I looked up, his eyes met mine and there was no need for words.

I was the first to break the painful silence. "Mark, am I going to die?" He didn't respond. I pulled away and asked again, "Am I going to die?" More silence.

Mark was my protector from the first day we met as freshmen at Whitworth College. The first gift I received from him was a porcelain figurine from the famous "Love is…" collection that was so popular in the '70's. It said, "Love is… always wanting to protect you." I knew he felt helpless. His fear was just as great—if not greater—than mine. We had survived a lot of obstacles in our 20 years of marriage, but this was all new territory.

I thought of the couples that faced similar circumstances and watched their marriages either thrive or crumble. *On which end of the spectrum would we end up?* The surgeon's words returned to haunt me: "You have breast cancer." I thought, *Cancer always happens to someone else, and now that someone is me.*

In the next room were our two boys, Jeremy and Jonathan, just 9 and 14. I staggered to gain control and left the comfort of Mark's arms to check on them. Jon was at the computer in the study and Jeremy was playing video games. Jon, our youngest, was the quiet one—I worried about him the most. Finally, I gathered up the troops and said, "Guys, I need to talk to you." They gave me "the look" that told me all I needed to know. Jon wrapped his arms around me and produced a piece of paper with the written words, "I love you mom, even though you have cancer."

To see the words "mom" and "cancer" in the same sentence produced a surge of terror. I held them close and said, "Guys, it's going to be okay. I am going to be fine." It was the Academy Award performance of my life—what an actress—I didn't believe a word of it. I must have sounded convincing because they left my arms and went back to their activities. But inside, I felt crippled by fear.

It was 3:45 p.m. on Thursday, March 21, 1996, and our life started down a new path—one I never imagined I would travel.

We spent the next few hours calling friends and loved ones, sharing our bad news. I wanted to call everyone and break the news myself—I didn't want them to hear it secondhand. The first on the list was my mom. She had anxiously waited for days to hear something... anything. The phone rang three times. Mom's sweet voice answered. *How was I going to say it? After all, Mom was diagnosed with breast cancer just five years before me.* She had to know—Moms always know these things. "Mom, I got the biopsy results back... I have breast cancer." There was a long pause. "Mom, are you still there?"

"Yes, dear, I'm still here. I was afraid it wouldn't be good news. Whatever you need I will be there. I can fly out tomorrow if you'd like?"

"Thanks, Mom, but we need to decide what we're doing first—we just found out. I'll give you a call in the next few days when we have a plan of action." I was fighting back tears. "I'll call you just as soon as we know, okay? I love you."

"I love you too, sweetheart. I'll tell Daddy and we'll put you on the prayer chain at church."

"That would be great, Mom, thanks!" I hung up the phone and burst into tears.

"I can't do this," I said, handing Mark the list of 31 names made up of family, friends, and co-workers. I was riding a roller coaster of emotions. One moment... laughing, the next... crying uncontrollably.

"Wait!" I grabbed the list back from Mark. I had one more phone call to make. I scoured the list. It was a teacher at Jon's school. His wife had cancer and she had survived against all odds.

"Yes, I found it! I just need to make one more call and you can do the rest."

Mark was riding the roller coaster with me, and we kept busy switching seats.

The phone rang several times, and then a voice I recognized answered. "Karen, this is Connie Pombo. I'm afraid I have some bad news. I was just diagnosed with breast cancer and your name came to mind. What should I do next? One second I'm crying, the next I'm laughing."

It was so comforting to hear her words. She was a survivor,

diagnosed late into the disease, and she was doing wonderfully. In fact, I guess you could say she was passionate about life. I had to hear someone who had been there and survived. It was as if she were pulling me up out of my pit of fear and despair with each word. Her calm, steady voice struck a chord deep in my heart, reassuring me that I would make it. This woman believed in a God of miracles. That's what I needed—a miracle! With each word, I started to feel hopeful. She gave me the name of her surgeon. She listened to my anxious thoughts as I rambled on incoherently. It was one long run-on sentence punctuated with, "I can't believe I'm having this conversation." She continued to listen. Finally, a pause... she jumped in. "Connie, I want you to feel free to call me anytime. I have some information I want to give you, but I will send that later. Steve and I will pray for you as soon as we hang up. Please know we do understand everything that you are going through. Give our best to Mark. I'll talk with you soon."

It wasn't a long conversation, but it was exactly what I needed to hear. She threw out the "lifeline" and I grabbed on: One fellow survivor sharing love, hope, and encouragement with another "survivor."

After that, Mark and I took turns making phone calls late into the night until every name had been scratched off the list. I looked at the names and realized these were the people who loved and cared for us. They were going to pray us through this ordeal one day at a time. We said a simple heartfelt prayer, "Lord, we don't know what the future holds, but we know who holds the future. Please give us the grace and strength we so desperately need."

We laid the list down, turned out the lights, and crawled into bed—we were beyond exhaustion.

The Days and Weeks That Followed

Good news travels fast, bad news travels faster. The very next day after we were put on the prayer chain at church, a gorgeous arrangement of roses arrived, a pastel palette of every conceivable variety and color: yellow, pink, lavender, peach, and white. The card simply read: "You are in our thoughts and prayers. We love you." If ever there was a perfect gift—that was it! I called it our "bouquet of life." It spoke volumes to me: With all the people who were holding us up before the throne of God, we no longer felt alone. By day's end, there were so many floral arrangements that we had to re-arrange the living room to accommodate them all. The phone rang incessantly and the backdoor stayed open for those who dropped off meals. Later, I wrote in my journal: "Like ants to a picnic they came, casseroles in hand." Food was so much appreciated because I had forgotten to feed my family in the flurry of activity that swirled around me. Some stopped by in person to encourage me. Unlike many in my situation, I appreciated those who shared their feelings. Those spontaneous moments of bursting into tears as they hugged me were precious—so real and genuine. It gave me a chance to cry again, but not alone—sharing pain "together" was very cathartic. A diagnosis of cancer affects everyone—family and friends. They too are dealing with their own feelings and adjusting to the diagnosis. The smallest gesture means so much, whether it's a gift of a card, hug, or freshly baked bread. The worst thing you can do is not say or do anything. I remember being in the supermarket a few days after my diagnosis, and a friend that I knew really well veered her shopping cart in the other direction in an effort to avoid me. I felt so alone, worse yet I felt like "damaged goods."

The Gift of Words

I saved the most meaningful cards as a reminder of what to say. The gift of your words will be remembered for many years after the diagnosis—choose them carefully. I saved the "best of the best" and still re-read them on occasion, usually when I need to write to someone who has just been diagnosed. After almost a decade, they continue to bring comfort, joy, and healing. One card, which arrived with a gorgeous planter, simply read: "Just to let you know we care and our prayers are with you." (Very simple, but meaningful. When in doubt, brevity is best.)

The most poignant gift came in a large Manila envelope, filled with handmade cards from my son's third grade class and a note from his teacher: "You are in my thoughts every day. I know this is a difficult time, but you will get through it. Call me for anything (Jonathan is doing great)!" She also delivered a basket of her favorite things: quiche, soup, freshly baked bread, and fruit. It was enough for several meals. It was so reassuring to know that Jonathan was doing so well in school. And the handmade cards from the children were precious—so honest, heartfelt, and innocent: "Mrs. Pombo—Hope you feel better soon. My grandma had 'kancer,' too. She's all better now."

It's very important to take your cue from the survivor—some days I just wanted to laugh and forget. Other days, I wanted to cry and remember. A favorite card came from a dear family friend: "Platitudes. You know... 'It's always darkest before dawn; every cloud has a silver lining, hang in there, keep your chin up'—the things people say when they don't know what to say. I hope to not make the same mistake! I know you'll make it through all of this because you have an indomitable spirit and a wonderful support system in Mark and the boys. So...'keep the faith, look both ways before crossing the street and, most of all, be sure to wear a hat so you won't catch a cold.'"

Journal Entry: March 21, 1996

The surgeon's words were quick and deliberate, like an axe to wood, splintering all hope: "You have breast cancer." I struggled to catch my breath. The surgeon was still talking but I didn't hear a word he said after the big "C" word. I hung up the phone and screamed, "What did I do wrong?" It was a moment frozen in time—my world has been turned upside down. Our lives will never be the same. Cancer has invaded our lives!

"But he said to me, My grace is sufficient for you, for my power is made perfect in weakness. Therefore I will boast all the more gladly about my weaknesses, so that Christ's power may rest on me" (II Corinthians 12:9).

What to Say and How to Help

The first stage of cancer is almost always shock. "It can't be happening to me!" The "shock" waves can last from several days to several weeks. Shock is actually a good thing in that it allows the body and mind time to absorb the pain in slow increments and adjust accordingly. During the first stage, emotions are running rampant. Important decisions need to be made in a relatively short amount of time. The caregiver, family, and friends are the most crucial during this period—keeping things running smoothly while the survivor learns ways of coping. Remember, there has just been an earthquake of seismic proportion, and aftershocks will last for weeks. It is a time of great emotional instability. You can never go wrong with the obvious—sending a card or dropping off a meal (but call first). Even the smallest gesture of love and kindness will help to stabilize the intensity of any lingering aftershocks. Always take your cue from the survivor.

Sometimes they will want to talk about their cancer, so be prepared to listen. At other times they may want to be diverted from it. However, do resist the temptation to "cheer the person up"—the ground has shifted beneath their feet—cancer is now the central focus. It is an exhausting time. Everything changes and priorities shift. Create a safe environment for the person to share feelings and don't be afraid to show emotion. I called my best friend in California right after I heard the devastating news, and immediately she sobbed uncontrollably. I cried right along with her. By the end of the conversation, we were both laughing hysterically. She rode the roller coaster with me. She felt terrible for not being strong. But our conversation was amazingly spontaneous, loving, and gut-wrenchingly real. It was just what I needed at the time. More importantly, don't give up! Everyone is different—what works for one person may not necessarily work for another. As a certified personality trainer, I know that each personality reacts differently to illness—some like to talk, talk, talk, while others need time and space alone to absorb the shock. Keep trying. Attitude and determination are important. Anything you do will be better than SILENCE.

Helpful Hints for the Survivor

- Say "YES" to offers of meals, cleaning, shopping, errands, and baby-sitting.
- Say "NO" to anything that makes you feel uncomfortable. My husband screened phone calls and visitors for the first few days until the shock wore off and my emotions stabilized.
- Practice deep breathing—in through the nose, out through the mouth.
- Keep a journal to record your thoughts. This was my best therapy, and the first gift I received. The inside cover simply read: "Start writing!" Try journaling your prayers to God.
- Turn a deaf ear to other people's cancer "horror" stories. You are a statistic of one. Don't feed your mind with negativity. Instead seek out survivor stories. Calling another survivor right after diagnosis was the best medicine of all, and started me on my journey of healing.
- Use life-affirming words. I call them "spiritual affirmations." The renewing of the mind is so crucial during this stage. I used several: I am perfectly healed; I am a survivor; I will live. Repeat as often as necessary.
- Don't apologize for your emotions. When you feel like crying, cry! If you feel like laughing, laugh! When you need time alone, say so.
- Telling friends and family. Although it was extremely difficult to share the diagnosis of cancer, it allowed others the freedom to offer their love and support. Friendships changed. A few friends slipped away, but the compassion of others more than made up for the loss.

Helpful Hints for Caregivers, Family, and Friends

- Always take your cue from the survivor. Remember, they have just received life-threatening news. It is a very vulnerable time. Some days they may want to talk about everything; other days they may fall silent. Be willing to

adjust your approach and expectations. Don't feel you need to respond to everything; just listen.
- The most important thing is to acknowledge the situation in a way that is most comfortable for you and is within the bounds of your personality. The worst thing you can do is to ignore them and not say or do anything.
- Respond from the heart and be yourself. The simplest expressions are the most meaningful: "I just heard the news; I want you to know you are in my thoughts and prayers."
- Keep visits short—no longer than 5-10 minutes—and always call first.
- Meals are a wonderful expression of love and support. Use disposable containers so nothing needs to be returned, and include any needed instructions. The goal is to make less work, not more.
- Show up with paper goods, paper plates, cups, napkins, and disposable silverware—anything to make the next few weeks easier for the survivor and the family.
- When going shopping, call ahead and ask if you can pick up anything. Your efforts will be much appreciated.
- Send life-affirming cards. They should express love, hope, and encouragement. Tell the person how much you appreciate them and what they mean to you.
- Plants versus floral arrangements? If in doubt, send a planter—they don't die—right away, at least, and it will be a constant reminder of your kind thoughtfulness for a long period of time.
- Personalized Gift Basket: Fill it with all their favorite things, including fun-to-read magazines, inspirational books, music CD's, funny videos/DVD's, and microwaveable popcorn. This is a great idea for a group gift.
- Offer to be the prayer coordinator updating the prayer chain at church via phone or e-mail. Some opt for websites with daily or weekly updates.
- Don't accept "No" as an answer. Look around and see what

needs to be done and do it: a lawn that needs mowing, errands to run, children to transport, laundry to be done, or books to be returned to the library. Your efforts will be much appreciated.

TWO

ANGER: WARNING SIGNALS

Everyone should be quick to listen, slow to speak and slow to become angry...
—James 1:19

The day of surgery, April 12, 1996, arrived—and with it, more decisions. Deciding on lumpectomy versus mastectomy was a nightmare. I tried to tell my surgeons that I was a very indecisive person. In fact, deciding on just the right parking space or what to fix for dinner was a big deal on most days. Worse yet, each one tells me exactly what I don't want to hear: "The survival rates are *almost* identical with either procedure." I tried every tactic known to medical science to get them to make the decision for me. In hushed tones, I would say: "If it were *your* wife, what would you tell her to do?" My pleas for help were ignored. Even my husband couldn't help me. No one wanted to be responsible for the outcome. It wasn't fair. After every surgical consult, I would leave with more tears—begging for someone to tell me what to do!

But that was behind me now. It was 6:00 a.m., the day of surgery, and we were heading for the hospital. The drive would take approximately 30 minutes—just long enough for me to change my mind about surgery again. *Was I making the right decision? Was it too late to call it off? Maybe I could call in sick?* No, all this is just pre-surgery jitters. After all, we're not talking tonsillectomy here. I was deep in thought—squirming around in the front seat of the car with indecision—when Mark's voice pierced the silence. "So what songs do you want played at your funeral?" I burst into tears. "My funeral? I'm having surgery today and you want to talk about my funeral?"

"Well, we haven't discussed it, and what if something happens?"

"Something like... death... you mean?"

"That's always a possibility with surgery; you know that. And we haven't talked about what you want."

My first thought was, *I'm too young to be planning my funeral—I'm just 40 years old—we shouldn't even be having this conversation.* Mark could see his timing was impeccable, as usual.

"I'm sorry. I can't make one more decision—it's just too much. Decisions about life, decisions about death, decisions about my funeral?" I was afraid to tell him that I was still undecided about lumpectomy versus mastectomy, and it was "surgery day."

"You're right—we don't need to talk about this now. If anything happens, I'll take care of everything."

That's all I needed to hear. "Wait a minute—you'll probably buy one of those super-fancy, mahogany, triple-lacquered coffins with all the bells and whistles, right? I don't want that. I want a plain coffin, a 'Celebration of Life' service, no viewing, a scholarship fund set up in lieu of flowers. Oh, and absolutely NO organ music—please!"

Mark was stunned. "For someone who doesn't want to talk about funerals, you sure changed your mind fast."

"Oh, one more thing. I want to be buried here in Pennsylvania. This is our home, where our boys grew up."

The whole planning took 30 minutes—perfect timing. The hospital was in view. *No turning back now.*

Once we were inside the hospital everything went quickly: check-in at admissions; wristband placement; changing into a flimsy blue-and-white-checkered surgical gown with tie strings in the back, blue hair net, and matching booties. Once settled in bed, the nurse took my vitals, started an IV, and hooked me up to monitors. I was ready—almost!

Mark drew the curtain open and said, "Look who stopped by?" It was Rick and Nancy—our dear friends from church. "We want to pray with you before surgery." They formed a circle around the bed, and we all took turns. During our prayer time, I felt a sense of peace—lumpectomy it would be.

After we finished, the gurney arrived and wheeled me down the vast white corridor towards the operating room. The Valium didn't work; I was talking incessantly with the orderly the entire way to the surgical suite. He asked, "What did they give you in your IV?" As we passed the last barrier—the surgical desk—I saw a stack of charts and next to them a single red rose in an empty lab container. I smiled. *Thank you, Lord, I'm in your hands now.*

Since it was a teaching hospital, there would be residents observing the lumpectomy procedure. It was a huge room and absolutely freezing. The nurses were floating around in their surgical garb making small talk. The surgeon appeared at my side along with his assistant—both dressed in all-green scrubs and masks. The Valium started to take effect—I could barely pronounce their names. The surgeon looked on as the technician strapped my left arm to the surgical board. Escape was definitely out of the question now!

The anesthesiologist was a first-year resident and looked younger than our 14-year-old son. *Oh, great—does he know what he's doing?* He reassured me that he was really good at his job. I had to wonder, *Was I his first patient?* I said a quick prayer. "Lord, please watch over him."

He asked me to count backwards from 100, 99, 98…

It's Over

I heard muffled voices. "Connie, wake up. Your surgery is over. Everything went fine."

Back where I started—same bed, same windowless cubicle. *"Did I actually have surgery? Maybe they didn't start yet?* The blood pressure cuff automatically tightened and loosened, making clicking noises. My throat felt raw and sore—it hurt to swallow. I thought, *Maybe they took out my tonsils instead!* I took a deep breath and then I knew—it felt like an elephant was sitting on my chest. I was smothered in thick bandages. *No, they didn't take out my tonsils!* In hushed tones I heard, "You can go back and see your wife now—she's awake." Mark walked into the little cubicle, bent over, kissed my forehead, and said, "Can I get you anything?" In a raspy voice, I whispered, "I'm hungry—what's for lunch?" Hunger pangs took over my fear of death. Unlike my neighbor who was extremely nauseous and kept the nurses busy running back and forth, I asked for food. My plea was granted. The nurse dutifully brought me a small plastic cup of ginger ale—no ice—slightly lukewarm, and a package of soda crackers. Perfect. I quickly gobbled them down and asked for the second course. Her disapproving look told me there would be NO second course. "I'm sorry—that's all we can give you—we have to see if they will stay down."

"I feel great—really—could I please have just one more?"

"No, absolutely not!" She was adamant.

Homecoming

I thought, *No food, no sleep—okay, no hospital.* My mind was made up.

"Mark, I'm ready to go now." I pictured a home-cooked meal waiting—just 30 minutes away. The thought of spending the night in the hospital with six other patients and a sheer curtain separating our beds made the choice an easy one. It turned out to be a great decision. But the off-duty surgical resident who was called back in after a 36-hour shift to sign my release papers didn't share the same enthusiasm.

On the drive home, we spotted the church van. Jeremy, our oldest son, was on his way to a weekend retreat. "Mark, stop the car—that's Jeremy." I jumped out and made my way to the van—waving with one arm. "Jer, it's Mom—I'm okay." We met in the median strip, exchanging hugs and kisses. "Have a great time at the retreat—I'm doing just fine. Have fun!" To see the worry melt off Jeremy's face was worth the early discharge and the problems it caused.

Once home, I made my way groggily upstairs and into bed. I wanted to take a nap before dinner. I felt little or no pain and the prescribed pain relievers weren't needed. I drifted off into a peaceful sleep. When I woke up, I glanced over at the digital clock on the nightstand—it had flipped to 7:06 a.m. I rubbed my eyes and checked it a second time. *How could it be morning? That means I slept 12 hours—impossible—I never slept that long in my life.*

The smell of freshly brewed coffee wafted upstairs, and homemade cinnamon rolls roused my senses. It was enough to move me out of bed and onto my feet. I gingerly made my way downstairs, where more flowers lined the bay window. The sense of God's peace and the love of His people filled my heart and our home. The prayers for a quick recovery were already answered. "Why didn't you wake me up?" I whined. Mom, who had flown in from California, was busy setting the table. "You were sleeping so soundly, we couldn't wake you up." (Later I heard that Mark didn't rest at all; he kept vigil all through the night, periodically checking on my breathing.) Dinner was now replaced with a scrumptious breakfast, complete with freshly squeezed orange juice.

For the next few days I rested. My surgery was uneventful and the pain was totally manageable. I dutifully did my exercises to regain full mobility, including the "wall crawl" each morning. The most difficult part was waiting for the pathology report. Each time the phone rang, I jumped to attention.

Back to Work

Going back to work was an easy decision; it would be a comfortable routine to get my mind off the impending pathology report. Getting up and being somewhere every day—I thought—would give me a sense of control and help bring my world back into focus. I resisted the idea of being referred to as a "cancer patient"—

and that's what I felt like. The feeling of wanting things the way they were before diagnosis was a false sense of security. Deep inside, the resentment started to build. *Why was this happening to me? After all, I did all the "right" things—I even ate organic alfalfa sprouts on rye bread, went to the gym every day, drank bottled water, and took a multi-vitamin. Wasn't that enough?* The more I thought of all the "right" things I did, the angrier I became.

Great News

I was back to work on Tuesday, April 16, four days after surgery. That afternoon I would hear the results of my pathology report. After lunch, the phone rang at my desk—I knew it was the hospital. A feeling of terror gripped me. "Connie, you're wanted on extension 121." I looked at the blinking light, thinking, *This phone call will change my life again.* My hands felt clammy, and beads of sweat formed on my upper lip as I reached for the phone. "This is Connie, may I help you?" I immediately recognized the voice on the other end. It was the breast-care coordinator. "Connie, I have great news—your lymph nodes are clean. There's no sign of cancer."

"So that means no chemotherapy, right?"

"Well, you need to speak with your oncologist about that. We worry about micrometastasis."

Now, why did she have to rain on my parade? I wanted some time to savor the good news. Micrometastasis is a possibility with any cancer. But reading it in medical journals was much more palatable than hearing the words "out loud" for the first time.

"I have two appointments coming up."

"That's great. It's always good to get two opinions. Keep us informed."

"Thank you for the wonderful news."

"You're welcome. It was my pleasure. Unfortunately, I have some other calls to make that aren't so good. I thought I would start with yours first."

Her words haunted me. For a split second I felt guilty for having "good news" and wondered about the other women who would be receiving life-altering words of another kind.

I hung up the phone and squealed, "My nodes are negative!" I jumped up and down and chanted, "My nodes are negative." Everyone gathered around to give hugs of affirmation and wish me well. Tears of joy streamed down my face. I wanted to savor the feeling for as long as I could.

More Decisions?

The sweetest words in the cancer survivor's dictionary are: benign, negative, clear, clean. They all mean the same thing—no cancer. Relief came in waves. But unlike the "shock" waves of fear, I rode the wave of hope for as long as I could. I felt relieved over the second phase of the cancer journey.

A decision still needed to be made regarding systemic treatment. Two appointments were scheduled with separate oncologists in different cities. My extensive medical research at bookstores and on the Internet led me to believe that two opinions were better than one. I felt compelled to arm myself with as much medical information as possible. Every afternoon, my car drove itself into the parking lot at the bookstore. My new form of recreation was sipping cappuccino and reading up on breast cancer tumors.

Many times the books never made it to the small table in the cafe. Instead I maneuvered them off the shelf and plopped myself down in the middle of the aisle. I was totally oblivious to customers who straddled my make-shift office in order to reach the other side.

Tumor Talks

Because of my medical background, I was not your "normal" patient. The first meeting with the oncologist was at a large teaching hospital. Mom came along with me for support. On April 22, 1996, at 11:00 a.m., armed with x-rays, a multi-colored tabbed syllabus, and a tape recorder, I was ready to plead my case on "how to save my life."

Dr. "G" made a lasting first impression as he entered the small sterile exam room. He extended his hand towards me and said, "First of all, I want to say how sorry I am for this unfortunate thing that has happened to you." Tears flowed freely. He was the first doctor to validate my feelings and to acknowledge me as a person—not a disease.

He glanced down at my large black notebook and said, "Well, I see you've done your homework. I wish all my patients were as well prepared."

His reassuring manner calmed my fears. I trusted him.

Of course, not all my physicians were as compassionate and understanding, so I was thrown off guard.

I prepared a list of questions—10 to be exact. He carefully laid the paper in my chart and turned his attention towards me.

"I will be happy to answer all of these after I get a little more family and medical history."

After asking permission, I put the tape recorder on the small desk in front of him. He didn't flinch. In fact, he asked me to make sure the volume was set loudly enough.

My assertiveness with doctors took years to acquire. When I first began in the medical field, I was timid and threatened by their knowledge and power. But now it was my life that was held in the balance, not a doctor's ego. One of my friends with breast cancer encouraged me to *shop around*. If a doctor won't take the time to listen, find another who will. She would say, "After all, Connie, it's your life we're talking about. Don't you deserve the best treatment possible?"

But with Dr. "G," I immediately felt a connection, a mutual understanding—he cared.

After he painstakingly reviewed my chart and answered every question to my satisfaction, he said, "I'll be back with my recommendations." The heavy metal door closed behind him. For the first time since my diagnosis, I felt like someone understood and actually took time to listen to "me."

Mom and I exchanged glances. "Why can't they all be like this?" My confidence and trust grew. "So, Mom, what do you think?"

"I think you are very fortunate to have found someone so competent and understanding."

After deliberating for what seemed like hours, Dr. "G" re-entered the small exam room. He pulled up a chair beside me. I took two deep cleansing breaths and prepared myself for the worst possible news.

In a reassuring voice, he said, "Your tumor has good characteristics. And because of the size, I am not recommending chemotherapy. You have a slow-growing tumor and chemotherapy usually works best on fast-growing tumors, so I'm recommending five years of a drug that will block the effect of estrogen on your tumor." Then he carefully explained how it worked.

That's all I needed to hear—the words "no chemotherapy."

"Thank you so much," I gushed enthusiastically.

"No, it's not me." He measured his words concisely, so I wouldn't misinterpret— "It's your tumor talking."

I didn't know that tumors could talk. But evidently mine did, and I liked what it had to say!

He then went into the details. "You have a good prognosis, about an 80-85% chance of living in the next five years." *Not bad*, I thought, *unless you're in the 15-20%.*

He wrote out a prescription for the drug that was given to women like myself with estrogen-dependent tumors in order to lessen the chance of "recurrence"—a word I didn't like to include in my medical vocabulary. In fact, I vowed never to say it out loud. He ended our time with the words, "I want to see you back in six weeks and be sure to call if you have any questions."

I grabbed the white piece of paper and gave him a hug.

"This is the best news I've had in weeks."

I'm not sure if I skipped down the corridor or ran, but my step quickly turned into a slow cadence as we filed past the chemo room. Mom felt my apprehension and said, "Come on, let's go have some lunch."

Quite honestly, I'm not sure if Dr. "G" knew how much he changed my life that day. He extended hope and healing with the simple gesture of holding out his hand. *Will anyone ever know how much the human touch heals the body and soul?* I felt strengthened with the power to go on. With God's help I could face this disease.

Good News/Bad News?

That very afternoon at 4:00 p.m., I had another consult with a different oncologist. I fully expected to hear the same good "news" I heard from Dr. "G," but nothing could prepare me for what I was about to hear.

The exam room was cold and sterile. Behind the door was a full-length mirror that hung crooked. I reached over to straighten it. *Who was that person staring back at me—I hardly recognized her—pale and sickly looking? It had to be the fluorescent lighting*—I hoped! In the corner was a small metal desk and above it, a handsomely framed picture of the human anatomy.

There was a brief knock at the door, and Dr. "H" entered the room. His starched white lab coat revealed his name in blue monogrammed letters—I struggled to pronounce it correctly. He struck me as a "just the facts" kind of man. I started to open up my voluminous notebook, but stopped as he shook my hand and introduced himself.

He looked through my chart in detail—flipping through pathology and radiology reports—and then announced, "I'm recommending six months of chemotherapy."

"You're recommending whaaaaaaaat? I don't understand. But I have negative lymph nodes."

I had the distinct feeling he was not accustomed to being cross-examined by a patient.

He then explained his reasoning. "The tumor is actually larger than originally thought. We always go with the pathology report rather than with the radiology report, so I'm recommending a course of chemotherapy."

I was reeling in disbelief. My good prognosis was suddenly in question.

"Wait a minute—HOLD ON—just a minute! I need some time to think this over. This is all new information to me." My chest tightened. I caught Mark's expression out of the corner of my eye—he seemed even more perplexed.

In a calculated tone, Dr. "H" said, "Cancer is *not* an exact science. There are *no* guarantees."

Confused and Angry

Part of me wanted to burst into tears—the other part was ready to explode. I was angry, resentful, and downright mad. Knowledge had replaced fear, but it did absolutely nothing to *squelch* my anger.

Before I could catch my breath, the nurse came in, ready to administer my first chemotherapy treatment.

"No thank you. I won't be needing that." I quickly picked up my things and said, "Mark, I REALLY need to go now."

He escorted me out into the waiting room, where the receptionist caught a glimpse of us. Peering up from the top of the counter, she said, "Wait, you need to make a return appointment."

"I'm sorry—that won't be necessary."

Mark took my arm and said, "Let's go!" My emotions threatened to devour me. Once safely inside the car I let loose—a deluge of tears poured out. I cried, "Lord, what am I going to do now? I'm so confused."

Roadblocks and Bumps in the Road

I realized later—much later—that anger is actually a powerful tool if directed properly. Up until that time, anger allowed me to do research, read up on cancer, make informed decisions, schedule and coordinate appointments, and feel in control. But now, my emotional tank was running dangerously close to empty. I had used up all my precious energy reserves. And yet another roadblock we weren't expecting loomed before us. A decision had to be made. I needed to stay calm so I could think clearly.

I prayed, "Lord, I feel so helpless. I can't do this on my own. Please guide me in the right decision. I need your wisdom. Please keep me calm."

Important decisions had to be made, but not in my condition. Anger clouded my thinking… the oncologist, nurse, and receptionist were not the targets. Plain and simple—I was angry because I had *cancer*. I covered it up by pushing it down and hiding behind an "it's okay" façade, but now I had to deal with it.

The scene in the doctor's office forced me to face my anger head on. The decision to have chemotherapy or not wasn't the issue—dealing with my emotions was the problem.

That evening, instead of searching for more knowledge at the bookstore or on the Internet, I opened up my Bible to Jeremiah 30:17. "But I will restore you to health and heal your wounds, declares the Lord…" Oh, how I needed to hear those words.

Instead of weighing the options of whether or not to take chemotherapy, I asked the Lord to search my heart. Saturated with medical knowledge, I needed His wisdom. Words flowed from my heart to my journal.

Journal Entry: April 22, 1996

Lord, I need to give up my life as I normally perceive it and view it as a moment-by-moment opportunity for you to work in my life. You love me and want to restore me to health. Calm my anger and allow me to rest in you. I can't do this on my own. My body and mind are just too tired. Give me the strength to accept whatever you have for my life. I am in your hands.

"The Lord is my strength and my shield; my heart trusts in him, and I am helped…" (Psalm 28:7a).

What to Say and How to Help

Many survivors find themselves angry, either about having cancer in the first place or what they might have done to cause it. Some are angry because of a bad experience with a doctor or other healthcare provider or even a family member or friend that was less than understanding or supportive. We all react to anger in different ways. My anger actually was a positive force in the beginning, fueling my efforts to make informed decisions regarding treatment. But hanging on to anger for prolonged periods of time is not productive: it drains you of much needed healing energy. My anger escalated out of proportion until my blood pressure skyrocketed.

Warning signals were being sent for weeks, but I wasn't listening to my body. Prayer, meditation, relaxation techniques, journaling, and music helped to bring my anger under control, so I was able to go off blood pressure medication and remain relatively calm throughout my treatment.

Helpful Hints for the Survivor

- Find someone you trust—a friend, pastor, or counselor—and share your feelings of anger. Talk about why you are angry, and discuss constructive ways of dealing with it. It was helpful for me to write a letter to myself. Afterwards, I destroyed the letter. The symbolic gesture allowed me to release the destructive feelings.
- Breathe. Breathe. Breathe. Take deep breaths—in through the nose—out through the mouth.
- Relaxation tapes. Listen to a variety until you find one that works for you. (Be prepared—after treatment you will NOT want to listen to them again!)
- Meditation and prayer. Take one verse or passage of Scripture, memorize it, and pray it back to God. I found the Psalms especially helpful (Psalms 90-100).
- Continue to get daily exercise, and connect with nature in some way each day.
- Visualization techniques. Find a place in your mind where you are completely at rest: a beach, a peaceful stream, a mountaintop, or a path in the woods. Close your eyes and bring yourself back to that place.
- Rest and relaxation. Suspend all activities that aren't absolutely crucial. Accept the help of others when offered. This is a time when you need to make yourself "top priority."
- Continue to write in your journal. Recording your thoughts on paper is great therapy and helps to release harmful emotions.
- Distraction. If you don't have a hobby, now is the time to find one. I took up photography and found that I was

passionate about it. Many survivors find hidden talent and abilities that they never knew they had.

Helpful Hints for Caregivers, Family, and Friends

- Allow the survivor to ventilate and express feelings of anger. Practice active listening; don't react.
- Realize there will be some backlash. Anger will pop up when least expected. Don't be upset by this or take it personally—realize that it is part of the journey.
- Deciding on a treatment plan is a very difficult time for the survivor. Expect frustration and feelings of anger. They may ask you, "What should I do?" I desperately wanted someone to tell me what to do. Unfortunately, you cannot. You can, however, offer your love, support, and encouragement. Whatever treatment the survivor decides on, be willing to support them in their decision.
- Medication may be prescribed temporarily to ease anxiety or, as in my case, rising blood pressure. Assure the survivor that this is all in an effort to bring healing to the whole body.
- Support Groups. Offer to attend a support group meeting with the survivor. Oftentimes all that is needed is someone to attend that first meeting with them. They will find out that they are not alone in their feelings and that others are going through the exact same emotions.
- Guard against false cheer. (This is harder for some personalities than others!) In an effort to bolster the survivor against negative emotions, you may be cutting off their attempts to express their innermost feelings. In doing so, you minimize or deny the reality of the situation.
- The two best words: "I'm here." These are the most supportive and comforting words you can say—they diffuse anger, provide comfort and love, and safeguard against hopelessness.

Helpful Hints in Dealing with Doctors and Your Healthcare Team

I thought it would be helpful to include a section here on the patient/doctor relationship—which is so vital. It is only natural that some doctor/patient relationships will be a natural fit, but other times they will be quite difficult. I found the following things helpful:

- Choose your doctors carefully. Selecting just the right doctor for you can be a painstaking process. View doctors as your partners in health. Let them know how much information you want and how involved in your care you would like to be. I decided early on that I wanted the best breast cancer surgeon available. I wanted to be sure he would "measure twice and cut once." I wasn't so concerned about bedside manner, but it was important that his surgical skills were excellent. However, I did want to find an oncologist who was compassionate, knowledgeable, and allowed me to partner in my care. It took time and it wasn't easy, but I found just the right one for me. The first three years after treatment, you will be seeing your oncologist on a regular basis, so make sure it's a good fit. The emotional benefits will far outweigh the time and effort spent in finding the right doctor.
- Thank you's. After working in the medical field for 20 years, I realized that doctors very rarely get letters of appreciation—mostly just letters of complaint. If a patient is dissatisfied with their care, they make sure their doctor knows about it! However, it is a rare patient who takes the time to write a sincere letter of "thanks." By the way, those letters get filed away in your chart—you will make a lasting impression. Doctors are people with feelings just like you. They can't always be everything you want them to be, but when they do take extra time and show compassion, let them know just how much it means to you.
- Not so happy—now what? If you find that you are displeased with your care, let your doctor know, but choose

your words carefully: humor helps—anger hurts. Many patients leave a practice and never say why they left. It can be very useful for a doctor and the practice—to find out why—so they can do better next time.

THREE

FEAR: CAN'T BE LATE TO RADIATE!

There is no fear in love. But perfect love drives out fear…
—I John 4:18

The decision was made. I would go with Dr. "G's" recommendation: five years of the estrogen-reducing drug instead of chemotherapy, and six weeks of radiation.

My first radiation treatment occurred on May 7, 1996. It would prove to be the testing ground for all my fears. If surgery made me anxious, radiation terrified me!

Ironically, I never had a mammogram, even after Mom's diagnosis of breast cancer, because I was frightened of radiation. Instead, I waited until the age of 40. By then I had already found the lump, and a mammogram was done for diagnostic purposes to confirm what I already knew—I had cancer. So how did I decide upon radiation as a treatment choice? There was no choice, really; it was given as part of treatment. If you elected for lumpectomy, radiation came as part of the package deal. I knew all that from my research, but somehow I managed to put it on the back burner, to be dealt with at a later date. *I would face it when the day came. And the day had arrived.* Simulation tests were complete. I received my badge of courage—tattoo marks on the chest wall that would guide the radiation beam to my cancer. The carefully calculated beams of radiation would accomplish their search-and-destroy mission to kill any remaining cancer cells.

Working full time in the medical field, only added to my burden of fear. I was surrounded by disease, sickness, and *death* every day. On my lunch break, I announced my departure by saying, "Can't be late to radiate. Gotta go, gotta go, gotta go!" I ate my tofu and alfalfa sprout sandwich on rye bread in the car on the way to the radiation center.

I distracted myself by repeating my "spiritual affirmations": *You are healthy; you are well; you are a survivor.* It would work until I arrived in the parking lot with its cleverly disguised entrance and well-defined privacy wall. For all intents and purposes, it looked like any other medical office.

Mark accompanied me to all my radiation appointments, holding on tightly to my hand so I wouldn't run away!

The first treatment was the most difficult. Mark asked if he could go back to the patient area to be with me, but the nurse politely said, "I'm sorry, you will need to stay in the waiting room." Mark shrugged his shoulders and let go of my hand.

I was escorted back to a small changing room where I put on a flimsy blue-and-white-checkered hospital gown—reminding me of surgery—and a pink robe that was more discreet and tied in the front. I waited in the "common area," a brightly lit space with skylights, tastefully decorated in earthen tones. A smattering of magazines lined the end tables, and other survivors sat quietly reading until their names were called. We all wore wristbands with our locker key attached. I closed my eyes and tried visualization techniques and listened to relaxation tapes.

My name was called, "Connie Pombo." It startled me. I had almost relaxed myself into a restful sleep. The "blue booties" managed to stay on as I shuffled past the other radiology technicians.

The pink robe—one size fits all—wrapped around me twice and threatened to slip off my shoulder as I struggled to keep pace with the technician. The long corridor, which I affectionately termed Fort Knox, loomed before me. The reinforced concrete walls lined with lead prevented the harmful radiation from escaping beyond its perimeter, and the sign "Caution Radiation Area," posted in black and yellow letters, alerted me to the fact that this was not your ordinary "tanning salon." In the middle of the large, sterile-looking space was an exam table that could be raised and lowered at will.

The technician took great pains to position me correctly, making sure to line me up with the radiation beam that would deliver the exact and precise amount of radiation needed to eradicate the cancer cells. Little conversation was exchanged until the technician said, "I'm sorry, but you can't have *this* during treatment" (referring to my headset and relaxation tapes).

I held on tighter, reluctant to surrender them. She saw the pained look on my face and said, "I'll just put these over here on the counter and you can have them back after your treatment is over." Stripped of my tapes, I was alone with my thoughts. There was nothing to do except wait. She took an unusually long time to line me up. "You need to relax, so I can position you correctly."

My body was resisting every move. The more I tried to relax, the more stiff I became. Every muscle group started to jerk and go into spasm. *How was I going to lay still for 15 minutes?*

"I'm sorry, this isn't working," I said.

My next impulse was to jump off the table and run as fast as I could into the parking lot—blue booties and all.

"I've changed my mind. I can't do this!"

She gave me a sugar-coated smile and said, "Oh, yes you can. You're just nervous, that's all. It happens with everyone. When you get through this first treatment, it will be so much easier."

I retreated into myself and accepted my fate. After all, this was my decision. *I prayed about it, others prayed for me, and this was where I was supposed to be—right?* Maybe I was over-reacting with first-day radiation jitters.

She reassured me that there was closed circuit television and that the technicians could see me, but I couldn't see them. *Oh great,* I thought. *So I really can't jump off the table and dodge radiation after all—they'll see me.*

"Oh, one more thing," she added. "If you happen to move out of the radiation zone, there will be an alert and radiation will automatically stop. Don't worry, we can hear you, so feel free to talk to us if you have a problem."

After delivery of that *great news,* she disappeared, making her way out of the room. I heard the vault-like door close behind her. I was terrified. I was left alone staring at the beam of light that would kill my cancer cells.

I thought, *Should I smile at the camera?* My arm was positioned over my head and it began to twitch—my muscles were in spasm. I wanted to scream, *"Wait, I'm not ready."* But it was too late, the radiation had started. Passing over me, making creaking-like noises, it was not at all what I imagined.

At one point, I thought, *What happens if I sneeze or jerk and the radiation beam misses and hits my eye? Will I go blind? How should I breathe? What if I breathe too deeply and the radiation beam pierces my lung? Will I get lung cancer?* I prayed, "Lord, I don't want to be here, but this is where my journey has led me, so make it fast." I reviewed in my mind what I had practiced, my spiritual affirmations. I envisioned the beam as a healing white light that took each dark cell—which represented my cancer—and dissolved it.

I kept repeating to myself, "This pure light is dissolving my cancer." The jerking movements stopped and my tired body finally relaxed. The actual treatment lasted no longer than five minutes, but it seemed like hours.

When I opened my eyes, the technician was back in the room with my chart. "You just finished your first treatment. That wasn't so bad, was it?" *Should I tell her the truth?* I kept quiet.

"You can go get dressed now and we'll see you tomorrow. Same time." I didn't feel any different. *Did I really have radiation?* I wondered what would happen if I didn't come back? *Was one treatment better than none?*

I changed as quickly as possible and made my way out of the building into the parking lot. Mark greeted me with a hug. "How did it go?"

"Fine, everything went fine. Do I look different?"

"No, you look the same."

I handed him a yellow sheet of paper with printed instructions that explained signs and symptoms to watch for, including slight tanning of the skin, and other possible side effects of radiation. I let Mark look it over; I avoided "warning lists."

"Mark, did it mention anything about glowing in the dark?" Finally, he was able to loosen into a smile and we both took a much needed "laugh" break!

Radiation Effect

The next few weeks followed relatively the same course. I left on my lunch break and returned, approximately 45 minutes later, just a little bit tanner than before. I experienced no unusual side effects or complications. The physical course of radiation was relatively easy. I put my fears on the back burner, where they simmered slowly until the last week.

The Beginning of the End

I worked full time throughout treatment, not missing a single day. During the last week I became extremely tired two hours after radiation, which was my only side effect. It was a "sick" kind of tired—unlike working in the garden or running five miles—and it was not relieved with rest.

During my last week of treatment, I shared the same time slot as Katie, a woman in her early 30's. Each day she brought a basket of freshly baked bread or muffins with homemade jam. Her hair was starting to grow back—peach fuzz was peering beneath her brightly colored baseball cap—a celebratory change from the customary wigs, scarves, and turbans. Strangely enough, none of us talked during our wait in the lobby area. But that day I broke the silence.

"I really like your cap. You wear a different one every day, don't you?" She looked up from her magazine and greeted me with a smile.

"Yes, I have quite a collection now. My oldest son started the whole thing, and then friends caught on. Now I have a room full of baseball caps." There was an awkward pause in the conversation.

"I'm just about done with treatment. How about you?"

"Actually, I just started radiation. I had a bone marrow transplant for inflammatory breast cancer. This is the end of my treatment—radiation." She didn't volunteer any more information. She must have seen the shocked look on my face.

"I know what you're thinking."

Was I that transparent? I thought.

"I'm an LPN. I told the doctors specifically that I didn't want to know any statistics or prognostic facts about my diagnosis. I don't read about my disease or look up things on the Internet. I have to get better for my family. I have five children and my youngest has Down's syndrome. She's three years old. Who's going to take care of her if something happens to me? Each day I have with my family is a gift. I don't allow myself to think beyond this present moment."

I was fighting back tears and nearly wore a hole in the carpet with my shoe... trying to keep from crying as she spoke.

She saw that I was visibly shaken. "I hope I didn't say anything to upset you." I quickly brushed away a stray tear from my cheek.

"No, you didn't. I'm just really tired of this place. This is my last week, and I can't wait for it to be over." I was afraid to make eye contact, so I changed the subject.

"I see you bring in something for the staff every day. Do you do your own baking?"

"Yes, I do. I love to bake. In fact, I thought about opening up a bakery at one time. You can imagine, with five children I never lack for taste-testers. The staff here has been so kind to me; I enjoy brightening up their day."

Our conversation was cut short. Her name was called. "It was good talking with you. Good luck with your treatment. I wish you well," she said.

I tried to respond, but the words stuck in my throat. The tears were too close to the surface. I feared with any slight movement they might come pouring out. I managed a weak smile and waved goodbye.

That would be the last time I saw Katie. Our time was rescheduled, so our divine appointments never coincided. There's not a day that goes by that I don't think of her in some way. No addresses, phone numbers, or e-mails were exchanged. It's as if we didn't want to know for fear of the outcome we both dreaded.

The Final Day

My last day of treatment was June 18, a Tuesday. It would prove fatal emotionally. I was physically weak and tired. The schedule of everyday treatments had taken their toll.

My name was called and the nurse led us back to the exam room, but not before getting my weight. As I stepped on the scales, she looked down at my chart and said, "We have the same date of birth. What a coincidence." Her cheerfulness immediately turned somber. "But you're so young." What she meant to say was: *You're too young to have cancer, and if you can get it, so can I.* That was the first time I realized there was a deep chasm between the "cancer" world and the "well" world. I reminded others of their own mortality—that they too could die. We struggle our entire lives building up walls to protect us from the thought of death, even to the point of not purchasing life insurance because we intrinsically think we are immortal. That day, I reminded her that our lives are temporal on this earth. Yes, you could get cancer and die. Yes, I am young and so are you. Cancer is no respecter of persons.

She led us into the exam room and said, "The doctor will be with you shortly." For the first time, I felt different for having cancer, and I realized that I would be treated "differently" the rest of my life.

I heard whistling in the corridor and the door swung open widely.

"Congratulations, you made it through treatment." announced the doctor. He held my thickened chart in his hands. Mark took a seat across from me. I sat on the edge of the exam table, feet dangling back and forth, watching the minutes tick away on the metal wall clock.

"So how are you feeling?"

"Fine, I think."

"Well, you completed your treatments successfully. I need to go over a few things before you leave. You need to be aware that there are some long-term consequences of radiation." *Oh, yes, the paper I didn't want to read at the beginning of treatment.* He started to enumerate the problem list and landed on a "trigger" word, a rare condition. I remembered it from my research days. He went on to explain the signs and symptoms and the eventual outcome—death!

Whaaaaaaaat? *Was that supposed to cheer me up?* I thought. Obviously, the doctor didn't know what a delicate state I was in emotionally. I knew he meant no harm; it was his job to inform me of possible side effects.

My eyes shot over to Mark. He knew I was cliff-hanging and this would certainly push me over the edge. Without a safety net, I fell. Plop! I checked out emotionally.

I don't remember leaving the building, walking out to the car, or what Mark said to me afterwards. I don't remember how I got home that night after work or how the celebratory dozen pink roses made their way from the car to the house. But I do remember going upstairs and lying down.

As I laid there, I thought of a class I took as a freshman at Whitworth College: Death in Contemporary Christianity and American Culture. It was a January term course, four hours a day for one month. We explored all aspects of death: physical, emotional, spiritual, and legal. We took several field trips including one to a funeral home, where one of our fellow students collapsed on the green tile floor when the embalming technique was carefully explained. Even then death didn't seem real to me, but now it loomed largely before me. I was facing my own mortality for the very first time.

The Unknown Future

I recalled the words of one surgeon, "Breast cancer scares me, you can have the best diagnosis and be dead in a year or have the worst diagnosis and live for 30 years." The first time I heard those words, I thought, *How comforting.* But he was absolutely right. Doctors are not God. They can only inform us about our disease and the potential side effects of treatment based on statistical data. The real answer to our future lies in God's hands. He is the one who has numbered our days. I had to wrap my heart around that thought and believe in God's promises. The choices given to me were just that—choices. God was the one who determined the outcome. My future was in His hands.

Journal Entry: June 18, 2004

Today was my last day of radiation. I feel numb. My bones are dry. I should be elated that treatment is over, but all I can think about is, *Did I do the right thing? Did I do all I could do?* I need to put a stake in the ground and not look back. I need to put my future in God's hands.

"Do not be anxious about anything, but in everything, by prayer and petition, with thanksgiving, present your requests to God. And the peace of God, which transcends all understanding, will guard your hearts and your minds in Christ Jesus" (Philippians 4:6–7).

What to Say and How to Help

Fear can creep in at any time during the cancer journey, but the two most crucial times are at the time of diagnosis and when treatment is over. Up until that time, there has been a constant stream of appointments, doctor visits, chemotherapy, and/or radiation treatments, phone calls, visits, and cards flooding in. When you're in treatment, you're too busy to think. Every day you have a schedule; the medical staff is attending to your cancer and your care. Then one day it's over—you're on your own. There's no instruction booklet on how to start your new life with cancer, just a release paper that says you finished treatment. While everyone else goes back to "life as normal," the cancer survivor is left in a holding pattern. During this time, fear and doubts linger. *Did they get it all? Will my cancer come back? Where do I go from here?*

One survivor summed it up this way: "I'm like the poster of the kitten dangling by its claws out on a limb." Some describe the feeling as if standing at the top of a cliff before being catapulted off the edge into the abyss. The waves of fear don't subside the day treatment is over. Worse yet, your family and friends are waiting for you to pick up where you left off. They are exhausted, and quite frankly relieved that it is finally over

For me, cancer treatment was like a part-time job, and then I was dismissed with nowhere else to go. The stress and fatigue wore me down. The fears I chose not to deal with during treatment, threatened to engulf me after it was over. *I could die from this disease.* Facing my own mortality was the first step in learning to LIVE again. We can go our entire life denying that death can happen to us until we are forced to deal with it. I felt like the scared little six-year-old girl who accidentally locked herself in her grandfather's shed. It was cold, dark, and terrifying, until my grandfather heard my screams for help and opened the door. The sunlight filtered back in and filled the dark, cold space. I walked freely into the sun. Guided imagery helped me face my fears of death—an inevitable part of life.

The spoken word becomes very important in the healing process. Since my diagnosis, I have come to realize just how important our words are. The Bible says in Proverbs 18:21a, "The tongue has the power of life and death… " There are "trigger" words—and they are different for every survivor. For me, radiation held great fear and continued throughout treatment until the final day, when words of healing turned into words of destruction. Since then, I have given seminars on "What to Say and How to Help," not only to cancer survivors and their loved ones, but also to physicians. We can all make a difference during this difficult time.

Helpful Hints for the Survivor

- Give yourself permission to talk about your fears with a close friend, a network of other survivors, or a support

- group. Talking about your fears diminishes their intensity and allows them to become more manageable.
- Seek help from a professional if you find your emotional and psychological needs are not being met by family and friends and your fear is escalating out of proportion. There are many groups and professionals that deal specifically with the emotional aspects of cancer.
- Nighttime fears. Lying in bed at night was the worst time for fear to creep in. During the day, I could keep busy, but at nighttime my fears closed in on me. In order for my mind not to wander the worry road, I committed to memory a passage of Scripture that I prayed back as a prayer: "The Lord himself goes before you and will be with you; he will never leave you nor forsake you. Do not be afraid; do not be discouraged" (Deuteronomy 31:8).
- The power of prayer. When we acknowledge our fear to God, who is all powerful, it loosens its hold on us. Seek out a prayer partner to pray with you through your fears.
- Relaxation tapes. I continued to use relaxation tapes before, during, and after appointments with doctors and at nighttime so I could drift off into a peaceful sleep.
- Breathing. Slow deep breaths—in through the nose, out through the mouth.
- Allow yourself to see cancer as the beginning of a new life—not the end of life. List all the things you have begun to appreciate since your diagnosis. I filled a page in my journal of all the little things in life that went unnoticed because I was just too busy: a magnificent sunset, children giggling on the playground, blue sky with white fluffy clouds, the taste of homemade vanilla ice cream, and a cool breeze on a summer's night. Your priorities and perspective will change drastically after diagnosis. Don't let fear hold you back from realizing your dreams and passions.
- Continue with your spiritual affirmations: *I am a survivor; I am healed; I look forward to each new day.*

- The friendship factor. After treatment was over, I found those who had stood by me during treatment suddenly disappeared. It was the most difficult part of cancer: lost or altered relationships. Some were just not able to cope with the possibility of my death. It was helpful for me to realize this was a part of the cancer experience—that they are also dealing with their thoughts of death. Mourn your losses and move on. Welcome new people into your life. The Lord gave me some wonderful new friends who brought joy, hope, and healing into my life.

Helpful Hints for Caregivers, Family, and Friends
- Provide a listening ear. Allow the survivor freedom to freely express themselves. Very few can get through the cancer experience without facing fear and anxiety. If they do remain buried, they will re-surface again at a later time.
- The gift of a wellness journal. I received two journals. One at the time of diagnosis, which said, "Start writing," and another one, which was given to me after treatment, that said, "To your new life!" Journaling is an excellent way to work through fear. It ultimately allowed me to start planning for the future with hope.
- Offer to accompany the survivor to follow-up appointments. The first few visits to the doctor after treatment are the most difficult. Fear starts to escalate, as the time gets closer. Let the survivor know you are available to go with them.
- If you are dealing with your own fears, don't burden the survivor. Consider seeking a support group for caregivers, a trusted friend, or counselor who is familiar with the emotional issues involving cancer.
- Offer to be an exercise companion. Exercise is much more fun and likely to continue when there is someone to offer encouragement. Physical activity is important in overall well-being and helps to reduce psychological stress.
- Continue to send life-affirming cards, letters, and e-mails—don't stop now!

FOUR

DENIAL:
GOING BACKWARD NOT FORWARD

For my thoughts are not your thoughts, neither are your ways my ways, declares the Lord.
—Isaiah 55:8

For the next three days after radiation, I remained in our bedroom counting the roses on the wallpaper—3,532 of the ugliest roses I had ever seen and yet I never noticed them before. Mark assured me that I was the one who had picked the wallpaper. But I denied it!

Life went on as usual for everyone—except me. The cards stopped coming. The phone stopped ringing. The meals stopped arriving. I wanted to go forward, but I slipped backward.

From the outside, it looked like life was "normal." Going to work was a real struggle, and each day was more difficult. What was once a great form of therapy, a daily routine and something to look forward to, soon became too much. I would retreat into the bedroom after work and listen to music or read. Mark had to assume most of the daily activities and, sometimes, all of them—taking the boys to their baseball games, doing the laundry, fixing dinner, cleaning the house, and grocery shopping. He did it all without complaining. He kept things running smoothly, while I lived in a haze of disbelief.

I was in total denial about my cancer. If at first it was shock about having it, learning to live with it was something I didn't know if I was prepared to do. I felt like a "victim" not a "survivor."

My first appointment with the oncologist after treatment was difficult. I realized there would be three years of non-stop appointments: monitoring blood work, x-rays, mammograms, tumor markers, and sitting in "cancer" waiting rooms. I willingly signed up for treatment, but not a lifetime of being looked at under the microscope, dissected, and probed. I carried my lab reports with me for that first appointment, and while waiting I looked down to see my name and the diagnosis on the same line: Connie Pombo, infiltrating ductal carcinoma, status post lumpectomy. *What? My name and cancer don't belong on the same line.*

Later, as I waited in the exam room, I thought, *How will my life ever be normal again?* I remembered back to the day when the technician made the tattoo marks on my chest for radiation. She made them very small—tiny dots in fact. I wondered at the time if she knew what she was doing. She had tears in her eyes as she was making them. *Wait,* I thought. *Shouldn't I be the one who is crying? What's wrong with this picture?*

"I'm making these very tiny because one day you won't want to remember this time in your life." She had that right! It was so much easier to deny the whole thing ever existed. Denial is the mind's way of not accepting reality—it worked. It got me through surgery and treatment, but now I was faced with the undeniable truth that I had cancer. I couldn't deny it any longer—I was holding back all the pain that I felt from the first moment I heard the words, "You have cancer."

One of the surgeons after my first post-op visit said, "I'm afraid you are in denial, and I predict that after treatment is over you will crash." It was inconceivable at the time that anyone could deny they had cancer—especially me—but that was exactly what I had done.

Facing the fact that cancer was my reality also meant I had to give up control. I *always* thought I had control of my life. That day in the exam room my illusion was totally shattered. The truth was I never had *control* to begin with. Hiding behind my notebook of lab reports and pathology reports, going back to work as if nothing ever happened, not wanting to continue with follow-up appointments for the years that lay ahead, was my way of taking control, but I had to let go. That meant grieving over all my losses—the loss of my health, my life the way I perceived it, the future that was uncertain, and my new reality that I had to accept.

The oncologist came in and greeted me in his warm but matter-of-fact manner and asked how I was feeling. "I don't know what to say. I'm still tired, but I don't feel 'normal'—I can't explain it."

He assumed a more professional stance, crossing his arms over his chest, and said, "You are going through a normal reaction after treatment. You need to be patient with yourself. However long your treatment was, your recovery will take that long or longer."

He listened to my heart and lungs, then looked over my blood work and said, "You're *perfect*. I'll see you again in three months."

That was it—I was an official patient/victim/survivor. I hadn't made up my mind which it would be. I got my calendar out and looked at all the X's that represented my life from the time of diagnosis to the end of treatment. They were crossed off one by one in black ink, each representing a day of my life with cancer that I fought so hard to deny. Now what was I going to do?

Trading Ashes for Roses

I drove home that evening, and Mark greeted me in the driveway. He held a red and blue envelope in his hand.

"What's this?"

"Open it up and see."

The envelope was heavy—it felt like airline tickets. I remember the nurse oncologist saying to me, "You should plan something special after treatment—something to look forward to—a vacation, a cruise, something just for the two of you."

Normally, I would have ripped the envelope open, waiting

breathlessly to see what was inside, but I opened it slowly and deliberately. There was a one-way plane ticket to San Francisco.

"Just one? Aren't you coming with me?"

"I want you to visit your folks in California. I called your boss at work and she's letting you take the next two weeks off. It will be good for you to get away. I called your mom and dad and they're looking forward to your visit. They want to spend some time with you.

"Are you trying to get rid of me?"

"No, honey, you need to take a break. Look what you've been through, you need some time to relax."

Ordinarily, I would have jumped at the chance to have two weeks' paid vacation and time to myself in California, but something didn't feel right. I was uneasy about the whole thing.

"Thank you, sweetheart. I appreciate all this, but what about the boys?"

"They'll be just fine. It's summer, and they have lots to keep them busy. Don't worry about us. Now go upstairs and start packing. You leave tomorrow."

While I was fumbling with the suitcase, the phone rang. Mark yelled upstairs, "Connie, it's Juanita. She wants to talk with you."

"Connie dear, I heard you weren't doing so well these days. I haven't seen you at church, so I decided to give you a call."

For weeks I had missed people calling me; now I just wanted to be left alone to pack.

"Oh, Juanita, I just haven't felt like myself lately. I'm sorry I haven't called. Mark is sending me to California to spend some time with my folks."

"Well, that's wonderful news. I didn't think working all that time during your treatment was a good idea. You must be exhausted."

I started to get edgy. Working was my way of denying that I had cancer, and one of the ways that I coped with my diagnosis. My routine made me feel "normal." Didn't anyone understand that? I was still holding on to that last tiny bit of control before I finally had to surrender it all.

"Oh, honey, I know exactly what you're going through. In fact, I prayed for you this morning. Just remember, Connie dear, God makes no mistakes, and one day you'll trade these ashes for roses."

"Juanita, you can't possibly understand how I'm feeling."

"Oh, honey, but I do. I was diagnosed with breast cancer 12 years ago."

I was taken aback. "How come you never shared that with me?"

"Well, I only tell the people that need to know, and I believe you needed to know. It came as such a great shock. My sons were all grown up—not young like your boys and that makes a BIG difference."

Fighting back tears, I said, "Juanita, I'm so sorry. It's so good to talk with someone who understands…. I mean really understands. Sometimes I want to forget I ever heard the words, 'You have cancer.' My life is so different—not what I ever imagined it to be. I feel like I've lost everything."

"It may seem like that now, but time has a way of healing our wounds. One day, you'll be able to share your experience with others and make a difference in their lives. Not that you will ever completely forget, but it does get easier. You're in my prayers every day."

Juanita prayed a short prayer and told me to look up Zephaniah 3:17 before I went to bed.

"Thanks, Juanita. I'll talk with you soon."

I sat on the edge of the bed and wrote down everything Juanita shared. Later I would find out so much more. She would become my "mentor in crisis"—traveling with me through the twists and turns that neither one of us ever expected. She was called alongside me to help me through this painful time. I so much needed to hear her words of encouragement: "trading ashes for roses." Would I ever be able to help someone with cancer the way she helped me?

Journal Entry: July 19, 1996

Juanita shared something with me tonight. She too had breast cancer—12 years ago. To think that I didn't want to talk with her.

Lord I know I'm a slow learner... REAL SLOW! Thank you for bringing Juanita into my life to show me the hidden blessings of this disease. Teach me what I'm supposed to learn from all this. I have received a gift tonight from a dear friend, and I can't thank you enough for sending her to me just when I needed to hear your Word.

"The Lord your God is with you, he is mighty to save. He will take great delight in you, he will quiet you with his love, he will rejoice over you with singing" (Zephaniah 3:17).

What to Say and How to Help

It is not unusual for cancer survivors to react to their diagnosis with denial. Our minds have a wonderful capacity for absorbing information when we are ready to accept it. The initial reaction is almost always shock, which is a form of denial. It keeps us in an anesthetized state—bubble-wrap protected—safe from the fears that threaten to shatter us. Eventually, the feelings of numbness and disbelief subside and the "postponed" psychological stress ensues. Everyone has an emotional timetable when it comes to absorbing new information, but especially when it comes to cancer and treatment. Oftentimes, I found myself saying, "I appreciate your concern, but I'm just not ready to talk about it." Taking care of my needs and trying to absorb the reactions of others was like walking a tightrope. Denial was so much easier because I could keep everything at a distance. I wanted things to be "normal" again, but I didn't even know what that was anymore. The most important thing you can do for anyone going through this stage of cancer is to listen and say, "I'm here."

Helpful Hints for the Survivor

- Realize that you are unique and so is your emotional timetable. Be patient and kind to yourself during this time.
- It's important that you share with those closest to you that you need their continued love, support, and prayers. Seek out emotional support systems at church, support groups, or with professional counselors who are trained in working with cancer survivors and working through the emotional

feelings related to a cancer diagnosis.
- Continue journal writing. Writing my emotions out on paper, when I wasn't able to express them verbally, eventually allowed me to see that denial was no longer healthy for me.
- Don't make major changes in your routine or add more stress. It's tempting to try to forge ahead and get back to a more normal routine, but keep in mind that your body is still adjusting.
- Seek out another survivor who has experienced your same feelings—someone to walk you through this difficult time. My mentor in crisis, Juanita Hiestand, was instrumental in allowing me to express my anxieties and my fear of death, which was at the root of my denial.
- Don't feel guilty for accepting offers of help or assistance, especially with daily chores, shopping, and meals. You still are finding your new "normal."

Helpful Hints for Caregivers, Family, and Friends
- Continue to support the survivor through your listening, love, and continued presence.
- Watch for verbal and nonverbal cues to determine when the survivor wants to talk. These cues are different for everyone.
- Be yourself and be natural. Don't try to be someone you're not. The survivor needs stability, not having to adapt to a "new" you.
- Encourage the survivor that they are not alone. This is not a private battle—you are there to provide a safe harbor. I always appreciated the fact that my husband said it was "our" disease. We were in it together.
- Resist being too cheerful, or saying, "Everything is going to be all right." This minimizes the survivor's fears and anxieties and doesn't allow them the freedom to share.
- Best words ever spoken: "I'm here!" In the roller coaster of cancer emotions, these two words are the most comforting.

FIVE

DEPRESSION: THE SKUNK TRAIN

My God, my God, why have you forsaken me? Why are you so far from saving me, so far from the words of my groaning?
—Psalm 22:1

    I left for California on Saturday, July 20, for what I thought would be two weeks of rest and relaxation. I was just beginning to see what I thought was the other end of the tunnel—LIGHT! I looked forward to the time away, hoping for a fresh perspective. I knew they had to call it "cancer recovery" for a reason.
    I felt relief just boarding the plane—finally, I would get a much-deserved rest. The spacious 747 took off as scheduled, and soon we were high above the clouds. I settled into my seat and flipped through some popular women's magazines to keep me company. The very first article I turned to was about "breast cancer and survival rates." There it was again—CANCER. I froze. We were at a cruising altitude of 35,000 feet and I still couldn't escape it.
    I knew better than to read anything about "cancer" in my fragile

state of mind. But the pages drew me in like a magnet. The plane hit turbulence, so the captain put on the "fasten your seatbelt" warning. The red flashing light should have been a signal for me to PUT DOWN THE MAGAZINE, but I didn't. The beverage cart rattled by me twice, but I missed the meal and I skipped the movie. I was making my would have, should have, could have list based on the article. It was absolute poison for my mind, but I continued in my reading frenzy: "The breast cancer survival rate has not changed in 20 years." I read on: "40,000 die each year." I closed the magazine and shut my eyes. I thought of Katie, the woman I met during the last week of radiation. I knew she wouldn't be reading articles on cancer. Absolutely not! She would be spending time with her family. She had learned the secret to living life with passion despite her pain. Her time was limited, but she saw it as an advantage, filled with concentrated moments of pure joy, simple acts of kindness, and time lovingly shared with family. *Would I ever feel that kind of joy again?*

Home at Last

I drifted off to sleep from pure exhaustion. When I woke up, the plane was preparing to land: *Please put your headrests in the upright position. Make sure your tray tables are securely fastened.* The flight attendant came around to collect our trash and I tossed away the magazine. The wheels touched down, not once, but a bumpy twice. I could see the sign as I peeked out the window. San Francisco International Airport—I was home at last.

As I walked off the plane, my parents waved in anticipation, but looks of concern filled their faces. We exchanged hugs and kisses. "Connie, honey, you've lost so much weight."

"A little I guess, I don't feel like eating." The medication to suppress my estrogen was causing hot flashes, night sweats, loss of appetite, and a depressed mood, but I thought it was all part of the price to pay for staying alive.

We made small talk on the way home, but soon I fell silent. After we arrived, I stumbled out of the car and made my way to the guest bedroom, dropped my luggage, and fell into bed, where I drifted in and out of a fitful sleep.

The very next morning, I could smell the aroma of freshly brewed hazelnut coffee, pancakes, and maple syrup. Normally, this concoction of smells would have moved me into the vertical position and led me right into the kitchen, but I couldn't get up. I felt chained to the bed. I laid there lifeless. Then Mom came in to "wake me up."

"I've fixed a nice breakfast, why don't you get up and have a bite to eat with us?"

"Thanks, Mom, but I'm not hungry."

"You have to eat something; come on... get up, you'll feel better."

My parents sensed something was terribly wrong. I did too, but I ignored all the warning signs. As I moved through the kitchen, I felt glad to be "home," but there really was something wrong. I was away from my routine. There was more time on my hands than I knew what to do with. How would I fill all the hours and not think about cancer?

"Come on, let's take a walk." *I barely had enough energy to get out of bed. How was I going to take a walk?*

"The fresh air will do you good. Dad needs to walk the dog, and we can all go together."

"No, I think I'll just go back to bed. I'm tired."

I wandered back to the bedroom, but couldn't go back to sleep. A couple of hours later, Mom came in to check on me.

"Connie, you need to get some exercise. You'll feel better."

She was right. I had absolutely no energy. During the night I developed a cough, and my lungs hurt to take in a deep breath. *What was happening?*

Mom finally managed to get me in the upright position and out the door. I muddled along, shuffling my feet through the almond orchards of Brentwood. We had lived in the same house—my parent's dream retirement home for two years—before we moved to Pennsylvania. Jon was just a baby then and Jeremy was five. It seemed so long ago. We had just returned from Italy as missionaries and were renting from my parents. The area had grown considerably since then. Tract homes replaced almond trees and the orchards were now sprawling communities filled with East Bay commuters. What was once familiar territory seemed like a foreign land—much like my cancer journey!

A Day Trip

After the third day, Dad thought a change of scenery might be in order, so we took a day trip up the California coast. We loaded up the car and headed north to Fort Bragg to ride the Skunk Train. I always wanted to do that as a child, so I was actually looking forward to the trip. We left early in the morning when it was still dark. I felt like Mom and Dad's little girl—all bundled up in the back seat with my pillow. As soon as daybreak approached we were nearing the ocean. It was a gorgeous day. The fog had lifted and the coast was breathtaking. I could smell the salt air, and I wanted desperately to dig my toes in the sand. We got out and walked along the beach for a while; the wind and the cold waters of the Pacific turned my toes pink, but it was invigorating. We still had quite a way to go to catch the Skunk Train, so we got back in the car and headed up the coast.

As we drove into the parking lot, I heard the train whistle blow loudly. I rolled down the window to take in the distinct smell of the redwood trees. A large crowd had already formed to board the train. Mom scampered out of the car to buy the tickets while we desperately tried to find a place to park.

"All aboard," said the conductor in a staccato voice. "Come on, we're going to miss it," I shouted. We were the last ones on before the train chugged off.

It was terribly crowded in the vintage coach compartments. We had a hard time finding seats, so we sat in different places scattered throughout the train. I caught one last glimpse of the ocean before we snaked our way through the dense forest.

The giant redwoods cast long dark shadows inside the train. A sense of panic came over me—I couldn't breathe! It was a feeling of being smothered. My heart raced and my chest tightened. The train went barreling through the towering redwoods as the whistle grew LOUDER and LOUDER. "Let me off the train. Please let me off," I screamed. There was a crack in the window a few seats ahead of me.

I climbed over the tops of the leatherette seats to get to it. Struggling to get the window down was futile. It budged just a few inches. My nose and mouth managed to sneak through the three-inch space to breathe in fresh air, but it wasn't nearly enough. I was suffocating! Finally, in total exhaustion, I slumped down in my seat and waited for relief to come.

Mom, who had seen me hurdling over the seats, came to my rescue. "Are you okay? What's wrong?"

"I can't breathe right; I think I'm going to die."

"You're having a panic attack."

"What? I've never had one in my life. Why is this happening now? What's wrong?"

Mom put her arm around me. "It's going to be okay. We're coming up to the station and we can get off. I'll get you something to drink."

The train was slowly grinding to a halt while passengers filed past until we were the only ones left in our seats. Mom and Dad helped me off the train as I staggered to the bench. Dad got us deli sandwiches and ice-cold lemonade.

"Do you feel better, honey?"

"I think so. I'm so sorry I ruined the trip."

"You didn't ruin anything. As soon as we get a bite to eat, we'll go home."

The L-O-N-G Way Home

It was late when we arrived back in Brentwood. The cool California evening was a welcome relief as I rolled down the window coming up the driveway. The crescent-shaped moon barely lit up the night sky. But it was quiet and peaceful except for an occasional cricket breaking the black silence. I crawled out of the backseat and somehow managed to find the front door, then dropped everything and made my way to the back bedroom where I collapsed.

That night would be the first of many nights when I woke up gasping for breath. I would sleep for a few fitful hours and wake up frantically—only to realize that the reality of my present darkness was worse than my dream. My clothes were drenched with sweat while I struggled for each breath. The same scene repeated itself over and over again. Mom would hear my cries, try to calm me down, and stay with me until I fell asleep. By morning, I was too exhausted to move.

During the day, I would sit in the living room and stare out the window. One afternoon, I caught a glimpse of Dad—he had tears in his eyes. I moved closer and put my arms around him. "Dad, what's wrong? Do I look that awful?"

"No, of course not. I was just thinking about you girls while you were growing up. I never spent enough time with you. Before I knew it, you were off to college, got married, and moved away. And now it's too late. I can never get back that time. It's gone."

"But Dad, you're spending time with me now." I gave him a big hug. "Dad, I know this is hard on you and mom—I never wanted to put you through this pain. I don't know what's happening to me. If I can't take care of myself, how am I ever going to take care of Mark and the boys?"

"It's going to take time. You're going to be all right—you just need to have faith."

The truth was that the combination of medication to suppress estrogen and all that I had been through—working full time through treatment and not taking time for myself—was manifesting itself in the form of depression. The classic signs were all there, but I didn't see them: loss of appetite, disturbed sleep, panic attacks, loss of weight, lethargy, and a feeling of hopelessness. It was made worse because I had a big empty space that I normally filled with work and other activities. Now I had too much time to just sit around and think. My vacation turned into a nightmare. The relaxation tapes, my journal writing, and prayer time were replaced with an empty vacuum that I filled with anxious thoughts.

Mom and I would take afternoon walks and pick roses from the neighbor's garden—they gave us permission! She listened as I shared my fears of the present and my hope for the future.

"Connie, I know it feels like you're on the edge of a cliff, ready to fall off. That's why they call it 'cancer recovery.' You need time to adjust, and that's what you're doing—recovering." I took some solace in her words. After all, she should know—she too was a breast cancer survivor.

I made the decision to leave California a few days earlier than anticipated. I needed to get back to my family. Healing was going to take time, and only the Lord could give me the peace that I needed.

As I readied to board the plane, I watched my parents wave a painful goodbye. Dad gave me the "thumbs-up" sign as tears rolled down his cheeks. I bravely waved back and headed down the "terminal" gate.

Journal Entry: Thursday, August 1, 1996

In the darkness of my deepest despair, you are there, God. Let me feel your presence. You are my Comforter. Comfort me. My brokenness and pain are all I have to give—that is my offering to you. You are the only one who can bring complete healing to my body. Make me whole again. I need to hope in you alone, God. Free me from this bondage of fear and death.

"May your unfailing love be my comfort, according to your promise to your servant" (Psalm 119:76).

What to Say and How to Help

There are two times in a survivor's life when they are most vulnerable to depression: right after diagnosis and then again after treatment is over. It's important to realize that fear, anxiety, and anger are all key players in depression. And unexpressed anger that is turned inward must always find expression: mine was depression. Try to be especially careful and alert to the signs of depression (see Appendix 3). Offer to help or seek help when needed. Usually this mood continues to improve over a period of two months. However, if symptoms continue to occur, seek professional help. Don't forget that physical health affects mental health and spiritual strength affects emotional strength. Is it any wonder that depression strikes at the end of treatment? Follow-up visits after treatment were especially difficult and brought back painful memories. And returning to work full time with the added burden of hospital bills pouring in just compounded the strain. A very painful realization was that my family members could not meet all my needs—their reserves had been used up. This is a time where connecting with some kind of support group—whether in your church or a local organization—is essential. Being able to talk to others who have been through the same experience and have overcome their difficulties gives a new hope for living.

Helpful Hints for the Survivor

- Realize that approximately one in four cancer survivors struggles with anxiety and depression after treatment. Know the signs of depression (see Appendix 3). If you experience any of the symptoms for more than two weeks, talk with your family doctor or a counselor experienced in working with cancer survivors.
- Join a support group. There are so many organizations that offer help for the survivor. Many churches offer "care groups" which provide both emotional and spiritual support. Contact your local hospital to find out about support groups that are offered. Also, check with the local chapter of the American Cancer Society, on the Internet, or with other cancer survivors.
- Exercise every day. Work up to 30 minutes three times a week. And connect with nature each day.
- Don't let people "unburden" on you. I had to stop people in mid-sentence, when I knew it was going to be yet another sad ending to a cancer story.
- Learn to laugh again. When you can start to laugh at yourself, then you'll know you are on the road to recovery. After one of my doctor appointments, I was in a rush to get to work and accidentally put my dress on inside out. When I got to work, someone had the kindness to share my error with me. I couldn't stop laughing. What a great feeling it was to laugh until I cried!

Helpful Hints for Caregivers, Family, and Friends
- Taking time. Realize that our bodies and minds are not completely separate. Cancer can take its toll not only on the survivor, but also on friends and loved ones. Don't ignore your own needs in the process of seeking help for the survivor. Cancer affects the entire family.
- Know and recognize the warning signs of depression (see Appendix 3). Offer to seek help or go with your loved one to a support group or see a counselor, physician, or pastor who is specifically trained in working with cancer survivors.
- Consider your own needs. Cancer places a tremendous strain on the entire family unit. Performing too many roles can cause a great deal of pressure on the family. Don't feel like you have to shoulder the responsibility alone. Learn to ask for assistance.
- Ask the American Cancer Society for names of local support organizations that are there to help you and your loved one cope with the emotional stress of cancer.
- Contact your local church. Many church organizations have "care groups," including depression support groups that are for cancer survivors and their families, to help them cope with emotional and spiritual needs.
- Check with your local hospital. Many programs are available for cancer survivors and their families in a group setting. They offer coping skills and practical tips.
- Continue to keep balance in your life: exercise, maintain a healthy diet, involve yourself in hobbies, and have an outlet for sharing your anxieties and fears.

SIX

ACCEPTANCE: THE OTHER SIDE

For I know the plans I have for you, declares the Lord, plans to prosper you and not to harm you, plans to give you hope and a future.
—Jeremiah 29:11

When Mark arrived at the Baltimore Washington International Airport, I think he was expecting to see the all "new" Connie, the one who was ready to pick up and start working again, and to see things in a totally different light. But the woman stepping off the plane looked far worse than the one he dropped off the week before.

He reached out to hug me, and I collapsed in his arms. There was no need for words. We each knew what the other was thinking. The ride home was quiet.

As we drove up the driveway, I saw that the backyard had been perfectly landscaped. It was immaculate, with new edging, colorful flower beds, and a beautiful pink dogwood tree in the center of the yard.

"What's this?" I said, pointing to the tree.

"This is our tree of life—a new beginning. We're starting a new chapter in our lives. Our faith journey begins here. God has brought us this far, and He's not going to leave us."

For the very first time, in weeks, I saw a glimmer of hope. It was brief, but it was there. Up until that moment everything had been in shades of gray, but now I saw color, a newness of life, for the very first time. It was a Technicolor moment—and I wanted to hold on to it forever.

The next few weeks allowed me to build on that glimmer of hope. It was between God and me now. Cancer allowed me to face my fears of death, anger, fear, denial, and now the deep bottomless black hole of depression. This was not the way I wanted to live what little time I had left on the earth—whether it was for one year or twenty.

One afternoon in late July, I looked out at the perfectly landscaped backyard with the dogwood tree growing so strong and tall, and asked myself, *What if I had a year to live? What would I do differently?*

I randomly wrote down 27 things I wanted to do before I died—that would become my passionate to-do list. They included such things as: take a family vacation to Maine, spend more time with family and friends, take a trip back to Italy, see our sons through safe passage into adulthood, go on a cruise, write a book, take a photography course, and #27, parachute out of an airplane!

When I finished the list, I laid it on the kitchen table. Mark read the list out loud and said, "I'm going to help you realize every one of your goals, and when that list is finished we'll write another one and another one—for the rest of your life."

For the very first time, I had hope: I could see life beyond cancer. It was no longer this bottomless black pit that led to death. Instead, I saw cancer as the beginning of a totally new life.

I remember the conversation I had with the oncology nurse. Her advice was simple: LIVE! She said, "Many women start entirely different careers; they do things they have always wanted to do: travel, go back to school, accomplish lifelong goals. It's not the end of life—it's the beginning. Cancer is not a death sentence." The conversation was the beginning of hope, and now I was holding on to it and making it my own.

Once you reach the bottom, there is nowhere else to go but up. Facing my own mortality was the beginning. Once you face your fears of death, you can start living again, but with new purpose and passion.

It was our 20th anniversary that year, and we had done nothing to celebrate. But we started to make plans to accomplish some of the things on my passionate to-do list. It was so much fun looking forward to each new day. Mark brought home some brochures from the travel agency, and we started to plan a three-day cruise to the Bahamas.

Planning for the trip—reading through the colorful brochures, imagining myself on white sandy beaches with azure skies and gorgeous sunsets, floating on the turquoise waters—was my exciting new form of visual imagery. And shopping became my new form of recreation, something I hadn't done in months. My focus had switched from death and dying to living life with passion. At one point, I thought, *It doesn't matter that we ever go on a cruise—it was just fun planning for it.* As the time came closer for departure, I realized the first of my passionate "to do's" was going to become a reality.

The panic attacks and depression that nearly consumed me became a faint memory. Occasionally, at work, I would experience some uneasiness when dealing with cancer patients, but it didn't overwhelm me. The feeling passed quickly. One of my doctors said to me early on in my diagnosis, "You know, Connie, we're all going to die some day." I knew that intellectually, but my heart couldn't wrap itself around the thought. It took time. Finally, I could put the reality of my death in perspective. Yes, it was true, I would die some day; but until that time, I was going to live. The fears did not automatically disappear, but when they did arise, I could deal with them.

I think we all long for certainty—the feeling of being in control of our lives—but cancer made me realize that was just an illusion. The whole time I thought I was calling the shots, I wasn't. My future was in God's hands. I believe because death is the great unknown, it holds the greatest fear. But I also believe that if God were to reveal heaven in all of its glory, a lot of us would be making a mass exit!

    The perspective cancer gave me on life was amazing. No one can take you to that place—it's a journey each person who lives with a life-threatening illness must travel—but I learned some valuable tools along the way. So much can be gained through suffering that even laughing takes on new meaning. I gave myself permission to fail. I didn't have to be perfect. As I looked through the brochures for our cruise, scuba diving caught my eye. I thought, *What if I can't do it? No problem, I'll try parasailing instead.*

    I suffered terribly from the "do it all myself" syndrome. Delegation was my new weapon for survival. The house didn't *always* have to be perfectly clean and in order. After all dust bunnies are harmless little creatures anyway! I eased up on my expectations of others and myself. While my passionate to-do list grew longer, my "I have to do it now" list got shorter and shorter. For the very first time, I made myself the number-one priority. The feelings of guilt gradually started to slip away. Even trips to the grocery store were something to look forward to. I splurged. If I didn't have a coupon, I bought the item anyway, even if it wasn't on sale. What a freeing experience that was. I ignored the generic paper towels and headed right for the beautifully decorated ones with flowers and nature scenes. I picked up "star fruit" for the first time and prickly pears (handle with care!). Picking out exotic new fruits and vegetables became an adventure. My shopping cart at checkout resembled nothing of its former self. Now that the house was well stocked with exciting new treasures—especially for the boys—I eagerly looked forward to our cruise.

Setting Sail

We set sail on Friday evening September 27 right at sunset. The Miami sky lit up, the sun filtering through the clouds. It looked like a jeweled crown. The joy and peace I found that night as we drifted out to sea was a new beginning.

An unexpected surprise was a cabin upgrade. We were treated to a spacious stateroom with a balcony—what a delightful shock! As we walked in the sun-filled room with its calming green and blue colors, there was a clear glass vase with two-dozen red roses and a bright silver bow. I ripped open the card peeking out of the bouquet: "To my one and only—to another 20 years together! Happy 20th Anniversary." The celebration of life was just beginning. We walked out on the balcony and watched the sun dip below the horizon. We were on our way.

The next couple of days were pure heaven. The beaches in Nassau were so warm and inviting. The water was crystal clear and the tropical fish that flitted in and out looked like toys, each capturing a new portion of my senses. We "tried" snorkeling instead of scuba diving. I performed the penguin walk getting into the water but, once there, a whole new world opened up below the surface. I saw everything with new eyes.

After a day in the sun, getting dressed for dinner was a real treat as I tried to wiggle into my dress with a blistering sunburn. We sat at the captain's table that first night with baked Alaska being flamed right there in front of us. Half the time I thought I was dreaming because it seemed too good to be true. How could two months make such a difference?

The celebratory atmosphere on ship was a reflection of how I felt about life. I would set our alarm clock to get up in time for the midnight buffet—I was afraid to miss out on anything. There were ice sculptures in the shape of mermaids, tables lined with desserts for as far as the eye could see, and flower arrangements that were a tribute to paradise itself. I didn't want the trip to end.

That evening in our cabin, Mark and I prayed, "Lord, thank you for this new beginning—a second chance at life—together." I loved the way that Mark always considered cancer "our disease"—not just my disease!

We returned home from the cruise totally refreshed. For the first time in months I actually felt like a survivor and started living like one. Although I returned to my work in the medical field, my focus was on living each day to the fullest. Each moment was precious. The spiritual affirmations that were begun in recovery continued, but the difference was that I believed everything I repeated: *I am a survivor; I am healthy; I am healed.* It was hard work in the beginning; I wondered if there would ever be a day when I would wake up and cancer wouldn't be my first thought. But the day came unexpectedly. I found myself getting ready for work and realized cancer wasn't even on my mind. I had crossed a threshold in my thinking. Each day I challenged myself to concentrate on the positive and to pray myself through my fears as they popped up.

The Race

An important part of my life before diagnosis was running and being physically active. I was always going to the gym and working out. Radiation drained me of energy and made my regular workouts impossible, but I resumed my routine slowly. The body is made for motion and my "engine" had been stalled long enough. Some days I had to drag my poor, tired body to the gym, but once there I got back into a rhythm. Whether our suffering is physical, mental, spiritual, or emotional, it is always stressful. And a typical response to suffering is to stop exercising. Those painful days in California were a reminder of what happens to the body when it lies dormant without exercise. I didn't move, but being depressed and staying in bed only served to make the situation worse. Exercising is the most important thing we can do for our bodies; it's also the first thing we give up when our body is in "crisis." The chemicals—endorphins—released during exercise actually aided in the recovery process. I also realized that depression didn't last forever. It was a byproduct of all that I had gone through—the anger, the fear, and the denial. They all kept my body stagnate.

One of the first things I did was enter a 5K race. I wasn't out to win a medal. I just wanted to feel my body move the way it used to. I wasn't the first to cross the finish line and, thankfully, I wasn't the last! I started to get back my equilibrium—exercise had become part of my daily routine once again.

Finishing the race was only the beginning of my newfound hope. Having been through the swirling black waters of depression—facing my fear of death head on—gave me new strength and determination to discover my passions. The support of family and friends who had been through the dark tunnel with me helped lead me to the other side.

Any tragedy in life can be a mixed blessing. For me it was a starting point to discover God's grace, the courage to uncover my worst fears, the strength to look beyond this present life, and the goals and determination to face the future. I wanted to help others face the race of their life—to share the journey to the other side—to live beyond cancer.

When I was in the dark place of my soul facing death, I read the book of Job because I could relate to his suffering. Job 23:10 says, "But he knows the way that I take; when he has tested me, I will come forth as gold." The purification process is not easy. It was the most painful part of diagnosis and treatment—depression and fears of death—but it shaped the way I would live the rest of my life.

Celebration of Life Day

On April 12, 1997, a bouquet of pink roses arrived on our doorstep. They were from a dear friend. The note simply read: *In Celebration of your new life—here's to another 5 years!* Each rose represented a new way of looking at life—the beginning of a lifelong journey of discovery. The bouquets would continue every year on my "Celebration of Life Day."

Part of the journey of acceptance and recovery is celebrating the milestones along the way. They are celebrated not only by the days, weeks, and months, but the moment-to-moment events that often go unnoticed by the average person: suddenly the sky is bluer, the grass is greener, and the air is fresher. For those who have not been awakened from the sleep of "ordinary living" to "extraordinary living," every day becomes a celebration of life.

Journal Entry: April 12, 1997

Today is my "Celebration of Life Day." The one-year anniversary of living life passionately! I watched Joni Eareckson Tada on the Billy Graham Crusade this evening. She shared how she had been in her wheelchair for 30 years. I listened intently to her testimony. She spoke with absolute clarity of heart: "Suffering is not to teach us *what*, but *whom*. It is designed to bring us closer to God." She went on to say that the lessons learned in her wheelchair were lessons she could not have learned any other way. It gave her a rock-solid foundation and faith in God—a precious joy for living. She expressed so eloquently everything my heart was yearning to shout. I will never know the "why" of my cancer, just as Joni will never know the "why" of her wheelchair. In my life, the "why" questions are now replaced with "what" do you want me to learn from this Lord?

"Trust in the Lord with all your heart and lean not on your own understanding; in all your ways acknowledge him, and he will make your paths straight" (Proverbs 3:5–6).

What to Say and How to Help

After treatment is over, whether it's surgery, chemotherapy, or radiation—or the BIG three—it is a tenuous time. I felt like a cat hanging by its claws on a tree limb, waiting for the limb to break or me to fall off. Up until that time, I concentrated on the healing of my body from cancer. But then I got my "get out of jail free" card. I didn't know what to do with it. Suddenly, treatment was over and I was supposed to go back to life as "normal." I didn't know what my new normal looked like. Cancer treatment can take a toll on the body—physically, emotionally, and spiritually—and it took a full year before I felt like myself again. Acceptance is part of the recovery process, but it continues throughout the rest of your life. In the beginning, it will be a daily battle: the thought of recurrence is always lurking. The first year, when recurrence is most likely, is definitely the most difficult. There will be doctors' appointments, tests, and the dreaded waiting for the phone call to receive the results.

The roller coaster of emotions doesn't end with treatment. Rather it ushers you into a phase of acceptance. Cancer is something you never forget, and no one expects you to forget it, even at the 5- or 10-year mark. But each survivor finds a way of coping with feelings of insecurity and loss. Those who have found the most meaning out of their diagnosis are the ones who have learned to give back in purposeful ways, to challenge themselves with activities that use all their gifts and abilities, and to find moments in everyday life that bring joy, laughter, and fun. There will be times when you feel like you're "cliff-hanging," especially during follow-up visits, anniversary dates of diagnosis, treatment, and surgery or the news that someone you love has been diagnosed with cancer. The moments I felt like I was perched on the edge of a cliff are a faint memory now. I have filled my life with the things that are most meaningful to me. Cancer may have robbed me of the innocence of infinite tomorrows but, instead, it filled my life with so much more than it took away. I now see each day as a precious and sacred gift, and I've learned to live in the present moment and to connect with my passions. The "new" normal of cancer is a joy-filled, purpose-filled life—a life beyond cancer that I've learned to live passionately!

Helpful Hints for the Survivor

- Curtail any activity that is not life giving and life affirming. Now is the time to take inventory. Decide which activities you truly love and which ones you can live without. If you are not passionate about any of them, scratch them off the list. Better yet, make a whole new list!
- Re-evaluate your relationships. Cancer alters relationships: some for the better, some for the worse. Health and healing are your new priorities now. And they are promoted through healthy relationships—those that bring you the most joy. Spend time with people who make you laugh and enjoy life.
- Priorities. Priorities. Priorities. List all your current responsibilities and decide which ones you would stop if you had a year to live. Let go of them now. Cancer brings into

focus what is truly important and valuable in life.
- Join a support group. You may find it's not for you and that's okay, or maybe you'll find the shared experience with others is exactly what you need. You won't know until you try. Check with the oncology department of your local hospital or with the American Cancer Society. Many online support groups also exist and I've listed other organizations in the Appendix.
- Connect with nature. Make sure you take time to walk outside, take in the fresh air, and connect with nature in some way daily.
- Learn to delegate. As women, we are the nurturers and caregivers, so we always put ourselves last. I used to feel guilty if I had to ask someone to do the laundry, wash the dishes, or clean the bathroom. It took time to let go of the guilt, but it's essential for survival.
- Listen to your body. I found that part of accepting my diagnosis was accepting my limitations. When I got tired, I rested. I allowed myself the privilege of taking a nap. Before I would push through the tiredness until I got everything done on my to-do list. Respecting and understanding my body and my energy gains and drains took time—it was a process. Remember, there is a difference between "doing" and "overdoing."
- Learn your body rhythm. If you're a morning person, save your most important tasks for the morning and vice versa. You will get much more accomplished when you work with your body rhythms.
- Nutrition. After I was diagnosed, I made an appointment with a nutritionist who was specifically trained in promoting health after cancer. I found that eating six small meals a day was better than three large meals a day. I changed the way I thought about food.
- Fear of recurrence. I have yet to talk with a cancer survivor who didn't worry about recurrence. The first three years are

the most difficult, but the focus has to be on living and not worrying. That means you have to be responsible about what you read, what you allow your mind to dwell on, what stories you listen to, and what you watch on television. It takes self-control. Ask God to be the protector of your mind.
- Continue to breathe. Before I used to count to 10 when I got angry, now I breathe—slow, deliberate, deep breaths—in through the nose, out through the mouth.
- Be a kid again! Part of acceptance is learning to live in the present moment and connect with your passion. Watch children play in the park. They aren't worried about tomorrow. They live in the moment. Keep a balance between work responsibilities and having fun.
- Prayer and meditation. The greatest healing comes from the inside out. Accepting by God's grace what we can't change. The "Serenity Prayer" continues to be part of my daily routine. It helps me to focus on the joy of the "present" moment.

Helpful Hints for Caregivers, Family, and Friends
- Keep the cards, letters, e-mails, and phone calls coming. The acceptance stage of cancer is the beginning of a new life. Like a toddler learning to walk, there will be falls and bumps along the way. Continual encouragement is needed.
- Express interest and concern, but take your cue from the survivor. I wanted to be treated "normally" again, but I was still struggling with emotional and physical issues. I appreciated those who would say, "How are you doing *today*?" It gave me the freedom to share what I was going through during that moment in time.
- Celebration of Life Day! Let the survivor pick the day. I used my surgery date, April 12. Others may choose to use the end of radiation or chemotherapy. A friend and I started the tradition a year after treatment. A Celebration of Life Day instills and serves as a reminder to thank God for all the

wonderful blessings of life.
- Allow for changes in mood and learn to be patient. The emotional and physical roller coaster continues for a long time after treatment ends. If you feel like your efforts to please are being rejected, do not be offended. Don't give up. Keep trying.
- Continue to help with errands, baby-sitting, and household chores, especially heavy lifting. Fatigue continues for quite some time. I felt frustrated not being able to keep up with things the way I used to. I appreciated the times when someone would ask if they could pick something up on their way to the store. I was so grateful for their kindness.
- Offer to accompany the survivor to their checkups. The first year is especially difficult. The worry starts to escalate as the day draws closer. It was always nice when someone offered the gift of their time or to have lunch afterwards—that way it became something to look forward to.
- Keep praying. I always appreciated the notes I received in the mail, even those that came months after treatment: "Just to let you know you're in my prayers." It was a blessed reminder that God's people were ushering me into the acceptance stage through their prayers.
- Don't wait for a special occasion. I received spontaneous and random acts of kindness for the first three years after diagnosis. No special occasion was needed—just "I'm thinking of you." One afternoon I came home from work to find a gift of homemade pasta and rolls, with a note that read: "For dinner tonight—thought you might need a break."
- Encourage activities that involve giving back. During that first year after diagnosis I started getting involved with the American Cancer Society and later giving seminars on "What to Say and How to Help." It helped not only with the acceptance of my diagnosis, but also to know that I was making a positive difference.
- Promote healthy living. I appreciated those who encouraged me to get back into an exercise program, to go back to the

gym, and to explore new ways of cooking. Their efforts helped me to think like a survivor.
- The gift of your time. To the survivor, time is a precious commodity. Those who offered to help me clean out the basement, go on spur-of-the-moment shopping sprees, or just take a walk were giving wonderful gifts of encouragement.

SEVEN

LIVING LIFE PASSIONATELY: A LIFE BEYOND CANCER

Cancer was a gift wrapped in ribbons of pain, fear, and doubt, but unwrapped itself into a life of unspeakable joy, purpose, and passion.

Cancer forever changed my life. I am not the same person—nor do I want to be. I like this "Connie" so much more. The journey that led to "living life passionately" was certainly not a path I would have chosen for myself. But it allowed me to face my own mortality, to ask myself the hard questions, and to see life as a precious and sacred gift. I received a newfound appreciation for life and all the precious gifts that it holds. I traded a life of pain for a life of passion.

Cancer was a definite wake-up call: life is short! It was an earthquake of seismic proportion. It shook the very foundation beneath my feet, and I staggered and fell many times, but I got back up. It caused me to evaluate my purpose in life, my goals, my God-given gifts, abilities, and talents. Was I using them effectively? The answer was "No." And now I had an opportunity to change all that.

The nurse oncologist was absolutely right: Some people start whole new lives, new careers, and fulfill lifelong dreams after being diagnosed with cancer.

It all began with the tree of life—a glimmer of hope—asking myself the question: If I had a year to live, what would I do differently? My passionate to do list was the beginning.

As I started achieving my goals and scratching things off my list, I not only gained strength and healing, but life came into sharper focus. You may be saying to yourself, "But I don't want a life-threatening illness in order to realize my passions." That's just it! You don't need to receive a diagnosis of "cancer" in order to realize your passions. Those of us who have received the news just get a head start. You have to want to change. And change is very difficult. In fact, it's downright scary. But after you have faced your fear of death, nothing is too difficult.

It's interesting that the Chinese symbol for crisis is the same as for opportunity. Cancer was an opportunity to change my life for the better—to do things I always wanted to do. What did I have to lose? The crisis of cancer allowed me the opportunity to look at life with a fresh new perspective. Only survivors gain true insight into how precious life is. Each day is a gift.

Those first few steps of transforming my pain into passion were difficult. But with every step, it became easier. I was moving in the direction of my passions. I wanted to make a difference in the lives of others—the way others had made a difference during one of the most difficult periods of my life. I wanted to inspire, encourage, and motivate others to transform their pain into passion.

Part of my journey in the recovery process was to take long walks. I would bring along my camera and take pictures. And then, when I received the photos back—I was amazed. Not only had the "lens of life" come into deeper focus, but the photographs I took were very healing. Photography is a moment caught in time—and that's just what I wanted—more time. Time to enjoy the gifts of today, to see our boys through safe passage into adulthood, and to experience life to its fullest.

As a way of giving back to those who had inspired me with their words of encouragement in letters or in cards, I made photographic greeting cards. "Cards by Connie"—born out of my passion for photography— was a way of giving back. Each time I sent a card to someone going through great pain, I was giving back—just as I had been healed by the words of those who loved and cared for me during the most difficult period of my life.

Volunteering to be part of a team for the American Cancer Society Relay for Life was another "step" I took willingly. The first time I took the field at Millersville University to walk the track for the 24-hour vigil, I was surrounded by a sea of other survivors—of every age group—who had followed the same path. As we crossed the finish line, walking the celebratory life walk, with pink and purple balloons floating through the air and the crowd cheering, I was so profoundly thankful for another year of life. At the finish line we received our survivor medal and one long-stemmed yellow rose—the symbol of friendship. These were my friends walking beside me. Although our lives were different, we had one thing in common—a golden thread that united us—our will to survive.

Each step of giving back was a step toward fulfilling my passions and reaching into the future with hope. I started giving seminars titled "When Someone You Know Has Cancer: What to Say and How to Help." To look out into the audience and to see heads nodding in affirmation was validation of our shared pain and, at the same time, a promise of hope for the future. I was making a difference with my life.

Going after the vision you have carved for yourself is not easy. There were definite obstacles along the way. It was difficult to see my progress at times. Then I was asked to share my journey— "Living the Passionate Life"—with a group of women at a retreat. My speaking engagements started to increase and Women's Mentoring Ministries was founded to share with other women the joys of a mentoring relationship and to help churches develop a mentoring ministry and build stronger leadership teams.

The uncertainty of where to go and what to do was now clear: I needed to leave the medical field to pursue my passion of speaking and writing full time. When Insight Publishing Company called and asked if I would be one of the co-authors of their book *Conversations on Faith* with Dr. Robert Schuller, Dave Dravecky, and Ann Jillian, I first thought it was a joke, so I hung up! When I realized it was the real deal, I felt honored to be able to share my story—to inspire, encourage, and motivate others to explore their passions in very practical and real ways.

"Living the Passionate Life" has now become my most requested retreat topic. To be able to speak, write, and share what God has done in my life is the most inspiring part of the journey.

The mentors who shaped my life have taught me the importance of living in the present moment and connecting with my passion. Juanita's words—trading ashes for roses—are etched in my heart and echo in my soul, but I did so much more—I traded a life of pain for a life of passion!

What to Say and How to Help

Cancer was the beginning of a new life path—a journey to discover my passions. Each day unfolds with new wonder, and another passion found. Do I think my passion reservoir will ever be filled? I hope not! Celebrations of life occur daily. Those of us who have confronted our fears of death and living with a life-threatening illness have been through a life-changing transformation: we are not the same as we were before. It is what allows us to "seize the moment," to embrace life with open arms, and to experience each God-filled moment with passion. Embarking on the passionate journey is the life I always wanted—a life beyond cancer!

Helpful Hints for the Survivor

- Make your passionate to-do list. Name at least 10 things and post them on your refrigerator to be reminded of them each day. Better yet, record them in your Celebration of Life journal. To get you started, ask yourself the following questions:
    - If you had a year to live, what would you do differently?
    - What would change in your life now in order for that to happen?

- What are some goals you can make in order for that to become a reality (name at least three)?
- If finances, time, or health were no object and no obstacles stood in your way, what would you do with your life?
- Enlist three joy mentors. These people will encourage you in fulfilling your passionate to-do list. They are life's cheerleaders. Think of the most positive people you know and write down their names.
- List three things that you would absolutely *not* change about your life.
- List three of your favorite activities and hobbies. Find time to do at least one of them each day.
- Write down at least one positive affirmation daily. Pass your Celebration of Life journal around to your family and friends and have them list at least three positive attributes about you. Read them—OUT LOUD—daily.
- Set goals. What do you want your life to look like one year, three years, five years, and ten years from now? If it's not on paper, it doesn't exist. Write them down in your Celebration of Life journal.
- What is the greatest obstacle standing in the way of you fulfilling your goals? Is it fear, resentment, discouragement, loneliness, worry, envy, guilt, or shame? Write them down and ask God to deliver you from them, so you can continue on your passionate journey.
- List three things that stress you out and list three things that counteract that stress, such as exercising, working in the garden, taking a friend out for lunch, shopping, reading a good book, or listening to music. Have a plan to counteract stress. Find a time each day to connect with someone you love and learn to say "No" to anything that doesn't contribute to your sense of well-being.
- Meditate: Learning to control your "inner dialogue" takes lots of practice. Schedule 10 minutes out of each day where you do absolutely nothing. Clear your mind of everything.

Whenever something jumps in, dismiss it, and learn to let go. Practice listening to your breathing by taking slow, deep breaths. You'll be amazed at how refreshed you feel after this exercise. Gradually increase the time as you learn to perfect the exercise.
- Journal your prayers to God. This is a great spiritual exercise. It allows you to hear God's voice and to keep focused. Allow God to speak to you through your prayers to Him.

Helpful Hints for Caregivers, Family, and Friends
- Be a joy mentor for your friend or loved one Encourage them in their desires, dreams, and passions. There is nothing you can do personally to change the course of their cancer, but there is so much you can do to help them achieve their goals and to make each day count.
- Help fulfill their passionate to-do list. Cancer threatens to attack one's self-esteem, in addition to threatening one's life. Make every effort to thwart hopelessness by helping to fulfill the dreams, wishes, and passions of the survivor. One of my passionate "to do's" was to write a book. It was a struggle to find the time to write, so my family made every effort to help by giving me the time, resources, and moral support needed to complete the journey.
- Encourage, inspire, and motivate the survivor into action. I'm so thankful that friends and loved ones didn't let me feel sorry for myself—they kept moving me forward. I avoided support groups as such, but others encouraged me to volunteer with the American Cancer Society Relay for Life, where I networked with hundreds of survivors each year. Another friend invited me to attend a Living Beyond Breast Cancer Conference, where I heard Dr. Susan Love for the first time. I found amazing support, and I was challenged by stories of strength and courage. It made me passionate about helping others find meaning through their cancer.

- The Weekend of Hope held in Stowe, Vermont, the first weekend of May, is a great place to start "new beginnings." The village of Stowe provides free lodging for cancer survivors and their families for a weekend filled with life-affirming activities, seminars, and workshops. It's an inspirational time and an ideal setting to start looking to the future with hope and passion (www.gostowe.com).
- Help the survivor envision the future. At one of the workshops I attended we were asked to write down what our ideal life would look like. What would get us up each morning and make us shout, "I love my life"? It was at that seminar that I carved out new life goals that were in tune with my talents, gifts, and abilities. I wanted to make a difference: I wanted to inspire, motivate, and encourage others through life's difficulties—transforming pain into passion. Allow yourself to be a catalyst for hope.
- Help create a journal of inspiration. To get me started, our small group Bible study wrote affirming cards and letters, stating one positive attribute they admired most about me. It started me down my path of finding my passion.
- Family and friends can have the greatest impact on the survivor's life through prayer. I'm so thankful to those who never gave up on me—those who encouraged me through the hard times, not letting me give up. They listened, encouraged, and inspired me to fulfill my dreams and passions. Remember: It takes a team effort!

EPILOGUE

"Time brings roses."
—Portuguese Proverb

Roses—what would my life be like without them? Whether a single rosebud or an entire bouquet, they have transformed my life. I can't go by one without admiring its beauty or smelling its sweet fragrance.

And I look forward to many more roses in my future... the corsage of pink roses I will wear to Jon's college graduation, the expectant bouquet of white roses on our 30th wedding anniversary, and the corsage of sweetheart roses I will wear to our son's wedding—and so many more roses—I have yet to imagine!

Cancer has allowed me to savor the roses of everyday life that would surely have gone unnoticed: a rainbow after the summer's rain, the wide paint brush strokes of the October sky, a cardinal in the December snow, and the first daffodils of spring. It's amazing to look back at life's transformation from victim to patient and now as a survivor celebrating life passionately!

My dear friend Karen said it best when she was diagnosed: "Why did it take a cancer diagnosis for me to realize what is really important in life?" It is a profound truth that no one can ever quite know the answer to—unless they have walked in our "rose" garden.

My mentor in crisis, Juanita, said, "One day you'll trade these ashes for roses." *Yes, Juanita, I know you're smiling from heaven—I finally got the memo!* Upon finishing the last chapter of this book, I went to Juanita's grave site and placed a single lavender rose on her headstone with a little prayer, *Your life was the best teacher of all—you taught me how to live. Thank you for showing me that every day I am alive is a day worth celebrating.*

The *ashes* of shock, anger, and fear have been traded for the unexpected *roses* of joy, purpose, and passion—a life beyond cancer—a passionate life worth living!

*Pleasant words are a honeycomb,
sweet to the soul and healing to
the bones.*
—Proverbs 16:24

APPENDIX 1

When Words Matter Most:
What to Say When Someone Is Diagnosed with Cancer

There is nothing worse than having a blank card staring back at you and wondering what to write. You will never be at a loss for words again. The following is a list of the most comforting, compassionate, and kindest words I ever received in card or letterform. Remember, the power of your words can make a difference in the life of the "survivor."

What to Say

- We love you and you're in our thoughts and prayers.
- Our thoughts and prayers are with you as you go through this time of hurt. If you need a listening ear—we're here.
- The Lord is not walking beside you at this time; He is carrying you.
- May you feel God's presence each moment of the day.
- What a beautiful gift you are to me—you are in my prayers.
- We touched the throne on your behalf that our Father in Heaven might send His comfort to you afresh in this time of deep need.
- May God's love and strength continually grant you complete healing and serenity.
- You are in God's care—"Hey, nothing but the BEST for MY friends!"
- You are not going through this alone.
- Sometimes God answers our prayers one day at a time.
- Life will be good again.
- I'm here!

What *Not* to Say

- *Breast cancer is incurable—right?* All things are possible—you have to believe from the moment you are diagnosed that

you will survive. This is a bump in the road, not the end of the road. I personally like to think of myself as "cured"—doesn't every survivor? Again, affirmation, hope, and love are the words that need to be heard.
- *My friend had breast cancer and died a slow, painful death—I hope that doesn't happen to you.* That comment put me into hiding for three days—I didn't want to see, talk, or be with anyone for fear I would hear something like that again. Leave your horror stories at home. Every survivor is a statistic of one—no one cancer is exactly the same. If you have a "survival" cancer story, share that one instead.
- *Call me if you need anything.* Instead, look for things to do. Combine activities and errands: if you're going to the grocery store, call and ask if you can pick up some milk and eggs. If you're going to the dry cleaners, offer to take things in or pick clothes up. If you're going to church, offer to take their kids. If you're returning videos, offer to get them something or drop theirs off. When mowing your grass, see if theirs needs mowing. (You get the idea!)

Things *Not* to Do

- *Don't disappear!* Worse than saying or doing the wrong thing is disappearing completely. A few of my friends completely walked out of my life—never to be heard from or seen again. I felt like "damaged goods." Whatever the reason, fear of losing you or facing their own fears of death, it's a devastating blow to the "survivor."
- *Phone calls.* Don't call unless you were part of the person's life before diagnosis. If you don't normally talk to them on a regular basis, don't start calling now. A card is always appropriate. It can be quite overwhelming when people start crawling out of the woodwork. (I received calls from people I didn't even know.) Try to keep life as normal as possible without a lot of extra drama.
- *Visits.* Don't just drop in. However, when dropping off a

meal, do just that—drop it off! Don't invite yourself in and ask for a medical update unless the survivor specifically asks you to, and then no longer than five or ten minutes—please! Resist the temptation to stay longer.

- *Meals.* Don't overdo the fats and sweets. A meal is always a kind gesture of love, but it should be nutritious. This is not the time to get out your gourmet cookbook with heavy sauces, fat-laden desserts, and empty calories. Think in terms of healthy soups, whole grain breads, salads, and fresh fruit.

APPENDIX 2

Helpful Things to Do

Although this book deals specifically with the emotional aspects of cancer: shock, anger, fear, denial, depression, acceptance, and living life passionately, the actual stages of diagnosis, treatment, and recovery require special thought and attention in order to help the survivor and their loved ones through the journey. I have included the most thoughtful actions that encouraged me during each phase of my journey.

For the Survivor, Caregiver, and Friends
How to Prepare for Appointments

- Doctor appointments. Ask for the last appointment of the day. That way the doctor is able to spend more time with you to answer any questions you might have without worrying about falling behind schedule.
- Fax a copy of your questions ahead of time, before your appointment, so the doctor can be prepared and you won't waste precious time.
- Always bring an "objective" third ear to doctor appointments. If that's not possible, bring a tape recorder. Always ask permission first. You can review the tape at home in a more relaxed atmosphere. If you have questions or don't understand something, you can call the doctor to get clarification. Make a list of questions, and don't be shy about asking them.
- Do your medical research, seek second opinions if necessary, and ask God for wisdom. No one is going to tell you what to do. Once you have arrived at the right treatment option for you, don't second-guess yourself.
- Be your own advocate. Make sure you get a copy of all your medical records. Oftentimes, I would arrive at appointments and they wouldn't have my lab work or pathology report.

After that, I carried all my reports with me. Every office is different. You may need to pay a minimal fee, but it is well worth it.
- Distract yourself. Have a book handy or a favorite magazine or hobby. Don't go to doctor appointments empty-handed—always have something to keep your hands and mind busy.

Things to do for the Survivor and Family During Diagnosis, Treatment, and Recovery
- Keep the meals coming. If someone is coordinating meals, make sure they know in advance your wishes, what time is best to deliver the meal, and if there are any dietary restrictions. If you are dropping off a meal, don't invite yourself in unless asked and then no longer than five or ten minutes. Always take your cue from the survivor. They may need to talk. Be sensitive to their needs.
- Send cards and letters. They should express love, encouragement, kindness, and hope. Tell the person how much you appreciate them and what they mean to you. One of the most powerful cards I received wasn't really a card at all, but a small insert that read: "Sometimes God answers our prayers one day at a time." The best cards came from my son's third grade class. Children can get away with honesty and the ability to bring a different focus—innocence.
- Prepare a gift basket: It can include a comforter, comfy socks or slippers, favorite magazines, books, music CD's or books on tape, herbal teas, and gift certificates. Gift basket boutiques can be found on the Internet or in the phone book. They can be tailored to fit the personality of the "survivor."
- Flowers and plants. They are a wonderful expression of caring; however, some are allergic to flowers or can't have them in the hospital. Think in terms of a planter or dish garden.
- Give restaurant gift certificates. We saved these for special occasions, to celebrate "good news"—like the day I

received my pathology report.
- Give childcare. Arrange for sleepovers if children are involved. Several families offered to have our boys for the evening. It was helpful—especially in the decision-making process when we needed time to pray and consider options.
- Run errands. Always call when you are going to the grocery store, dry cleaners, or pharmacy. Ask if there is anything you can pick up on your way, and offer to drop it off.
- Make use of prayer chains and websites. Many churches and individuals develop websites to keep family, friends, and church members informed about treatment dates, progress, and follow-up. If you know someone who specializes in using computers, by all means ask. They would be honored to be able to help out. Delegate one person to keep the prayer chain informed.
- If you are a co-worker, talk to your employer about donating sick days and vacation time to the survivor so they can concentrate on healing. The gift of time is the greatest gift of all.
- Organize fund-raisers. Oftentimes, for whatever reason, the expenses incurred in treatment are not covered by insurance, or there may be a lack of insurance. It takes someone to organize the event (raffles, dinners, auctions, sports tournaments, sub sales, or car washes). The financial strain of cancer treatment can be just as devastating as the diagnosis. This is a terrific way to lessen the burden.
- Don't forget the caregiver. They are carrying the emotional burden and doing most of the physical work around the house. If the caregiver is also the breadwinner, they have been working double shifts, at work and at home. Offer to take over some activities around the house that they don't have time for. Make a healthy snack basket for them to munch on when they are running low on energy. Offer to exercise with them or get them a gym membership. Be there as a support and offer to listen. Find out their favorite

activity and surprise them with a gift certificate. Watch out for signs of depression. Cancer affects the entire family—not just the survivor. Offer your love and support and to take over some of the neglected activities—especially yard work. Most of all, pray for the caregiver and everyone in the family—this is the most important thing you can do.

APPENDIX 3

Signs and Symptoms of Depression

Not everyone who is depressed experiences every symptom. Some people experience a few symptoms, some many. Severity of symptoms varies with individuals and also varies over time. If any of the following signs are noted for more than two weeks, please seek the help of your doctor or a professional counselor.

- Persistent sad, anxious, or "empty" mood.
- Feelings of hopelessness, pessimism.
- Feelings of guilt, worthlessness, helplessness.
- Loss of interest or pleasure in hobbies and activities that were once enjoyed, including sex.
- Decreased energy, fatigue, being "slowed down."
- Difficulty concentrating, remembering, making decisions.
- Insomnia, early-morning awakening, or oversleeping.
- Appetite and/or weight loss or overeating and weight gain.
- Thoughts of death or suicide; suicide attempts.
- Restlessness, irritability.
- Persistent physical symptoms that do not respond to treatment, such as headaches, digestive disorders, and chronic pain.

APPENDIX 4

Scripture Readings
Verses of Comfort and Hope

"Look to the Lord and his strength; seek his face always" (I Chronicles 16:11).

"The Lord is a refuge for the oppressed, a stronghold in times of trouble" (Psalm 9:9).

"But I trust in your unfailing love; my heart rejoices in your salvation" (Psalm 13:5).

"The Lord is my rock, my fortress and my deliverer; my God is my rock, in whom I take refuge. He is my shield and the horn of my salvation, my stronghold" (Psalm 18:2).

"For he has not despised or disdained the suffering of the afflicted one; he has not hidden his face from him but has listened to his cry for help" (Psalm 22:24).

"Be strong and take heart, all you who hope in the Lord" (Psalm 31:24).

"Though he stumble, he will not fall, for the Lord upholds him with his hand" (Psalm 37:24).

"Why are you downcast, O my soul? Why so disturbed within me? Put your hope in God, for I will yet praise him, my Savior and my God" (Psalm 42:5).

"God is our refuge and strength, an ever-present help in trouble. Therefore we will not fear, though the earth give away and the mountains fall into the heart of the sea, though its waters roar and foam and the mountains quake with their surging" (Psalm 46:1–3).

"Cast your cares on the Lord and he will sustain you; he will never let the righteous fall" (Psalm 55:22).

"He will cover you with his feathers, and under his wings you will find refuge; his faithfulness will be your shield and rampart. You will not fear the terror of night, nor the arrow that flies by day, nor the pestilence that stalks in the darkness, nor the plague that destroys at midday" (Psalm 91:4–6).

"You are my refuge and my shield; I have put my hope in your word. Sustain me according to your promise, and I will live; do not let my hopes be dashed" (Psalm 119:114, 116).

"Though I walk in the midst of trouble, you preserve my life; you stretch out your hand against the anger of my foes, with your right hand you save me" (Psalm 138:7).

"So do not fear, for I am with you; do not be dismayed, for I am your God. I will strengthen you and help you; I will uphold you with my righteous right hand." (Isaiah 41:10).

"When you pass through the waters, I will be with you; and when you pass through the rivers, they will not sweep over you. When you walk through the fire, you will not be burned; the flames will not set you ablaze" (Isaiah 43:2).

"But blessed is the man who trusts in the Lord, whose confidence is in him. He will be like a tree planted by the water that sends out its roots by the stream. It does not fear when heat comes; its leaves are always green. It has no worries in a year of drought and never fails to bear fruit" (Jeremiah 17:7–8).

"The Lord is good, a refuge in times of trouble. He cares for those who trust in him" (Nahum 1:7).

"Peace I leave with you; my peace I give you. I do not give to you as the world gives. Do not let your hearts be troubled and do not be afraid" (John 14:27).

"I consider that our present sufferings are not worth comparing with the glory that will be revealed in us" (Romans 8:18).

"Praise be to the God and Father of our Lord Jesus Christ, the Father of compassion and the God of all comfort, who comforts us in all our troubles, so that we can comfort those in any trouble with the comfort we ourselves have received from God. For just as the sufferings of Christ flow over into our lives, so also through Christ our comfort overflows" (II Corinthians 1:3–5).

"But thanks be to God, who always leads us in triumphal procession in Christ and through us spreads everywhere the fragrance of the knowledge of him" (II Corinthians 2:14).

"For God did not give us a spirit of timidity, but a spirit of power, of love and of self-discipline" (II Timothy 1:7).

"Cast all your anxiety on him because he cares for you" (I Peter 5:7).

APPENDIX 5

How to Enjoy a Positive Attitude for Life

ACCEPT:
Christ's forgiveness
Receive the joy of salvation,
Count your blessings and...

LIVE:
Look for good in everyday life
Do not act like a victim,
Be a blessing and...

LAUGH:
Recognize that attitude is a choice,
Believe there is good in everyone,
Know that where there's life, there is...

HOPE:
Believe that what you do matters
Share your faith in God
Give God glory, praise Him and...

SING:
Put your difficulties into perspective
Appreciate the value of today
It rarely, if ever, physically hurts to...

SMILE:
Do what you can, in the place that
You are, with the time that
You have with...

LOVE:
Prioritize—what is the worst
That will happen if you don't
Get it done today?...

Surround yourself with positive people
And take time to...

BREATHE!

—Tricia Keener Miller
November 16, 1962–January 28, 2001

RESOURCES

American Cancer Society
1-800-227-2345
www.cancer.org

Breastcancer.org
www.breastcancer.org

Cancer Care
1-800-813-HOPE
www.cancercare.org

Cancervive
1-800-4-TO-CURE
www.cancervive.org

HealthWeb
www.healthweb.org

Living Beyond Breast Cancer
610-645-4567
www.lbbc.org

Mayo Clinic
www.MayoClinic.com

M.D. Anderson Cancer Center
www.mdanderson.org

MEDLINEplus Health Information
www.medlineplus.gov

Mothers Supporting Daughters with Breast Cancer
www.mothersdaughters.org

National Cancer Institute's Information Service Center
1-800-4-CANCER
www.nci.nih.gov

National Coalition for Cancer Survivorship
www.cansearch.org

OncoLink
www.oncolink.com

Pennsylvania Breast Cancer Coalition
1-800-377-8828
www.pabreastcancer.org

Strang Cancer Prevention Center
www.strang.org

Susan B. Komen Breast Cancer Foundation
1-800-462-9273
www.komen.org

The Humor Project
518-587-8770
www.humorproject.com

TheBreastCareSite.com
www.thebreastcaresite.com

Well Spouse Foundation
1-800-838-0879
www.wellspouse.org

Imaginis: The Breast Health Resource
www.imaginis.com

Y-Me National Organization
1-800-221-2141
www.y-me.org

Young Survival Coalition
212-206-6610
www.youngsurvival.org

RECOMMENDED READING

A Journey Through Cancer, Emilie Barnes with Anne Christian Buchanan (Harvest House Publishers, Eugene, OR).

A Season of Hope: Daily Encouragement for Your Fight Against Cancer, Michael S. Barry (Cook Communications, Lee Vance View, CO).

Be a Survivor: Your Guide to Breast Cancer Treatment, Vladimir Lange (Lange Productions, Los Angeles, CA).

Breast Cancer, What You Should Know (But May Not Be Told) About Prevention, Diagnosis, and Treatment, Steve Austin, N.D., and Cathy Hitchcock, M.S.W. (Prima Publishing, Rocklin, CA).

Dr. Susan Love's Breast Book, Susan M. Love, M.D. (Perseus Publishing, New York, NY).

Grace for Each Hour, Mary J. Nelson (Bethany House Publishers, Bloomington, MN).

Heaven, Joni Eareckson Tada (Zondervan Publishing House, Grand Rapids, MI).

Hope in the Face of Cancer: A Survival Guide for the Journey You Did Not Choose, Amy Givler, M.D. (Harvest House, Eugene, OR).

Hope When It Hurts: A Personal Testimony of How to Deal with the Impact of Cancer, Larry Burkett with Michael E. Taylor (Moody Press, Chicago, IL).

Living Beyond Breast Cancer, Marisa C. Weiss, M.D and Ellen Weiss (Times Books, New York, NY).

Love, Medicine and Miracles: Lessons Learned about Self-Healing from a Surgeon's Experience with Exceptional Patients, Bernie S. Siegel, M.D. (HarperCollins, New York, NY).

Not Just One in Eight: Stories of Breast Cancer Survivors and Their Families, Barbara F. Stevens (Health Communications, Inc., Deerfield Beach, FL).

Nothing to Fear: The Key to Cancer Survival, Larry Burkett (Moody Publishers, Chicago, IL).

Spinning Straw Into Gold: Your Emotional Recovery from Breast Cancer, Ronnie Kay, (Fireside, Simon and Schuster, New York, NY).

The Breast Cancer Book of Strength & Courage, Ernie Bodai, M.D., F.A.C.S. and Judie Fertig Panneton (Prima Publishing, Roseville, CA).

The Breast Cancer Survival Manual: A Step-by-Step Guide for the Woman with Newly Diagnosed Breast Cancer, John Link, M.D. (Henry Holt and Company, New York, NY).

When God and Cancer Meet, Lynn Eib (Tyndale House Publishers, Carol Stream, IL).

When God Weeps: Why Our Sufferings Matter to the Almighty, Joni Eareckson Tada and Steve Estes (Zondervan Publishing House, Grand Rapids, MI).

WORKS CITED

Note to Readers
Ries LAG, Eisner MP, Kosary CL, Hankey BF, Miller BA, Clegg L, Mariotto A, Feur EJ, Edwards BK (eds). *SEER Cancer Statistics Review*, 1975-2002, National Cancer Institute. Bethesda, MD, http://seer.cancer.gov/csr/1975_2002/, based on November 2004 SEER data submission, posted to the SEER web site 2005.

Epilogue
Portuguese Proverb, source unknown.

Appendix 3 – Emotional Signs and Symptoms of Depression
National Institute of Mental Health. Depression. Bethesda (MD): National Institute of Mental Health, National Institutes of Health, US Department of Health and Human Services; 2000 [reprinted 2002; cited 2004 January 26]. (NIH Publication Number: NIH 02-3561). 23 pages. Available from: http://www.nimh.nih.gov/publicat/depression.cfm

Appendix 4 – Scripture Readings
Scripture taken from the HOLY BIBLE, NEW INTERNATIONAL VERSION® Copyright© 1973, 1978, 1984 by International Bible Society. Used by permission of Zondervan Publishing House. All rights reserved.

Appendix 5 – How to Enjoy a Positive Attitude for Life
Tricia Keener Miller, "How to Enjoy a Positive Attitude for Life," (1962–2001). Used by permission.

Printed in the United States
38315LVS00002B/104